UNCOVE
Y
INVITA
TO COME
HOME

FOURTH
CHAIR

ANNE BARBOUR

The Fourth Chair
Uncovering Your Invitation to Come Home
www.annebarbour.com
www.thefourthchairbook.com

Copyright © 2022 by Anne Barbour

Published by The Core Media Group, Inc., www.thecoremediagroup.com.
The author is represented by WordServe Literary Group, Ltd.,
www.wordserveliterary.com.

Cover Design: Anne Barbour & Nadia Guy
Cover photo provided by Tatyana Kim via Canva.com
Interior Design: Nadia Guy

ISBN 978-1-950465-56-9

Printed in the United States of America.

Contents

For John–
My husband, friend, and love.

Introduction

I've had a recurring dream for decades. I'm walking through my house and happen upon a passageway I had never noticed. When I follow it, I discover portions of the house I had no idea existed, and it's magical. I am instantly elated, thrilled to find what was right under my nose. The discovery is always a massive upgrade, so I can't wait to find my husband to tell him that apparently, we have been confining ourselves to living in the mudroom of a palatial estate! I usually wake up not long after the "big reveal." The effects of the dream linger in the form of a bittersweet heartache. I get a strong sense that I am very near something that would catapult life into a new stratosphere, if only I could see it.

I spent many years feeling just that way as a follower of Jesus Christ. I wasn't sure what it was, but I knew there was something I wasn't "seeing" and that if I *could* see it, it would ignite the life I was certain I was meant to live as a child of God. I knew my faith in God was rightly placed. I also knew there was far more to my attachment to Him than I was experiencing. So I began to explore my immediate surroundings, confident the answers I sought were within view. And God, in His time and way, started giving me sight for the treasures that were all around me.

Then one day, a picture of four empty chairs dropped into my mind. They were arranged facing inward and fairly close together. Somehow I understood that three of these chairs were for the Triune God—the Father, the Son, and the Holy Spirit—and the remaining chair was for me. What on Earth was the significance of that? I wanted to know.

For many years now, God has been using this simple scene to introduce me to Himself and what it means to be His child. He's shown me the way to the vibrant, fulfilling life that I was missing, even though I had belonged to Him for so many years. He deconstructed the faulty systems of belief that were responsible for the disillusionment I felt and then rebuilt a reliable foundation. More than anything, He drew me to Himself and helped me discover and enjoy the greatest treasure a human could ever possess.

If you can identify in any way, I believe a read through this book will help bridge the gap you might feel between the life you're currently living and the one you feel might be just out of view. Maybe you do not know God at all but are curious. Or like me, you may recognize the need of a fresh look at the God you are already in relationship with. I believe what follows in these pages will serve you, regardless of where you are in your journey.

God promises abundant life to His children, both now and forever. Something as simple as a good, long look at four chairs—and who might be occupying them—could be the very thing God will use to reveal the richness of life to be found all around you. That's just what He has been doing for me. Not one large or small element of my life has remained unchanged as I have pressed into the Lord, begging Him to "tell me everything" about the picture He dropped into my mind. I got (am still getting) far more than I imagined. I believe you will too. If you have never occupied the fourth chair before, you will not believe what is in store.

> *"No eye has seen, no ear has heard,*
> *nor the heart of man imagined,*
> *what God has prepared for those who love Him."*
> —1 Corinthians 2:9

Part 1

The Invitation
What Is Man That You Are Mindful of Him?

"What is man that You are mindful of him,
and the son of man that You care for him?"
—Psalm 8:4

In two short phrases, the psalmist David revealed that not only does God think about us; He cares about us. That came right on the heels of David's declaration of God's preeminence, His power over His enemies, and His creative prowess (see Psalm 8:1–3). David elevated God as high as his language would allow and then said succinctly and accurately, "What is man that You are mindful of him, and the son of man that You care for him?" It's as if he said, "How on Earth could this be?" He's caught up in the wonder of what appears to be a great discrepancy.

Any conversation we have about our proximity to and interaction with the living God has to be couched in light of His altogether otherness. We must be caught up in the wonder of Him, just as David was. We must "see" the discrepancy between the greatness of God and the smallness of man, or we'll miss the indescribable gift it is that

He would care for us.

To be caught up in the wonder of His affections is to be on the precipice of experiencing something grander still because God, interested in expressing His affections, extends an invitation to you and me to draw near to Him. The whole of The Bible bears witness to a series of invitations to humankind to engage with our Maker. He's always had this in mind.

The book of Genesis cuts to the chase from the first chapter. We're told God created the heavens and the Earth and everything within them. He created a man and a woman in His image, and gave them stewardship of the Earth. And He walked with them *in the garden in the cool of the day"* (Gen. 3:8). There, in the garden, God and the humans He created enjoyed reciprocal, harmonious relationship. Everything was just as God intended. The experience of living utterly fulfilled was theirs. Life was literally perfect—until Adam and Eve disobeyed God.

Our experience of the world and of people bears such a faint resemblance to those initial days in Eden. We have no frame of reference for that idyllic scenario. But God's intentions were in no way diminished when sin entered the world. The impediments to healthy relationship were considered and addressed by God, making it possible for us to know Him, even as we are known by Him. Sin, and the inevitable separation from God it would cause, did not catch God by surprise or unprepared.

I wonder if consciously or otherwise, we think about Eden as a fabulous ideal, but one destined to fail, and therefore a mistake in its inception. It lasted such a short time. Perhaps God held in the wings a backup plan "in case of emergency." But such a consideration would open up the possibility that God could make a mistake.

"You have worked wonders, plans formed long ago with perfect faithfulness." That's what Isaiah had to say about the reliability of God's master blueprint (Isa. 25:1, NASB). God Himself declared His creative acts to be good and very good (see Genesis 1:4,10,12,18,21,25,31). And the psalmist sang in Psalm 18:30 (AMP), *"As for God, His way is blameless. The word of the LORD is tested…"* Over and over, the Word makes plain that God is the essence of perfection.

What happened in the garden did not knock God off His game. He didn't head back to the drawing board because He didn't make a mistake in the first place. He intends and desires that we are in active relationship with Him. Those desires are fixed in the heart of God, never to be undone. Whether or not we find ourselves in relationship with our Maker depends entirely on us. He cares for us. The invitation is before us—and always has been.

Chapter 1

The Four Chairs

Introducing the Metaphor

I came to faith in God as a young girl, carefully watching the example of my parents, who deeply loved God. I was six years old when I prayed a prayer, asking Jesus to "come inside of my heart," believing I was in need and that He was the only One who could save me. I never questioned that decision, nor was I exposed to the possibility that it might not be the right one. I was immersed in all things "Christian," spending the bulk of my family life in community with those from our little church. It was, for me, idyllic and wonderfully insulated.

By the time I was sixteen, my parents had divorced and our beloved church family, in response, had basically withdrawn. I figured we must have been too much trouble, and because of that we were allowed to slip outside the ranks of that fellowship. I was a young girl in crisis, bewildered, disillusioned, and deeply depressed. I experienced the remainder of my teen years essentially numb. Internally, those years were deafeningly quiet. There was no "sound" to life anymore. I was getting out of bed every day and "doing" my life, but I did not feel present in any substantial way. It was if my actual life were a dream and I was in it, yet somehow also outside it. I would lose memory, unable to retrieve any content of what transpired over multiple days. This is a common occurrence for a person suffering with deep depression.

I was not sure about my proximity to God during those years; I spent most of them not having a sense of His presence. What I do remember very clearly is having one phrase emerge out of the perpetual fog. It became a lynchpin that would keep me attached to life. I did not hear the voice of God, yet this phrase was deposited to me as if He'd spoken it: "I am real." I anchored to those three words, and God began, very slowly, to build on them a construct (a building from the foundation up) that would withstand the inevitable storms that would test it in the decades to follow. It would equally stand up to my many attempts to rule my own destiny.

A few years back, I watched a scene in a movie depicting an astronaut in space, floating a great distance from his ship, but still tethered to it. A malfunction had occurred that shot him away from the ship. He was adrift until a solution could be found to retract his tether. He was immediately in touch with how much or little faith he had in the provision of the tether, no longer having the security of a firm hold of the ship. That scene struck a chord in my soul and jettisoned me decades back to my youth and to those many years of disorientation.

The constant tension of knowing God existed, but not being able to feel His presence, was the thing that would take my young heart to the brink of despair. It was also the thing that kept me from going over that brink. I understand now that God was allowing me to experience the reliability of that tether. It never broke, frayed, or became compromised in any way throughout those dark years. I had to understand that, regardless of how I felt or what I would experience in the years to follow, my attachment to Him was unbreakable. I belonged to Him, and He was not letting go.

There was also an aspect to life, after the breakdown of my family and extended community, that caused me to appreciate simple things in a way I couldn't have previously. There was an awe and wonder factor, a little like finding a green shoot springing up on a hillside stripped bare by fire. It appears profoundly vivid in that context, where normally you would never even see it. I would experience that whenever I felt seen by someone, or when a person might try to push through the "no solicitors" vibe I put out. I might not allow them in, but I would feel something a little miraculous in being noticed and pursued. Sometimes I would allow them access to me. From those with good intentions (sent by God, I am sure), I would receive a tangible expression of the love of God—a drink of water for a parched young girl.

Teens have loads of drama swirling in and around them on a normal day. Most of mine was internal, buried in the caverns of my psyche. But I can tell you, when I had occasion to be with a family who appeared intact and happy together, my heart would ignite with hope—and then, a second later, plummet in despair. I would have the same reaction when I saw friends enjoying one another. I was inordinately needy and awkward but determined not to appear vulnerable. I had a fortified wall built around my heart, while having eyes peeled, looking for relationship.

For reasons only God can know, it suited Him to dismantle my young life and begin building from the ground up. I can say without hesitation that I am grateful to have had those years for the treasure they yielded. They came and went as they did for my good and for His glory. *"And the rain fell, and the floods came, and the winds blew and beat on that house, but it did not fall, because it had been founded on the rock"* (Matt. 7:25).

I give you that look into my young life because I see an overt link between that pivotal phrase "I am real" and the impact of a picture that emerged in my mind thirty-five years later.

Several years ago, while I was hiking in the hills behind my home in Southern California, I remember being conscious of a mental picture of four chairs. They were facing each other in a small circle. They were empty, but the idea was clear: three were designated for God, in the persons of the Father, Son and Spirit, and one was reserved for me personally.

When the picture came, it could come in only through the grid of my beliefs, which were built on the certainty of the reality of God. For all that remains weak in my faith, I do not doubt that God is real and present. That made this picture immediately plausible.

I am an extremely pragmatic person. I also have a very active mind hardwired with an "app" that produces streams of analogies. So I "see" pictures all the time. I am better able to think through things if I can find some sort of scenario that might represent the thought I'm mulling over. Most of the time, I don't give undue credence to these pictures. Plus, every analogy has a point where it fails, serving a thought only so far.

But occasionally, some of those pictures linger. By that, I mean they might reemerge several times over a period of weeks or even months. When that happens, I pay close attention and begin to pray, asking God to speak to me if there is something He's meaning for me to know. To that end, I open my Bible looking for stories from passages that might help me find a principle to either refute or substantiate the picture in my mind. I also weigh the substance of that picture in light of what I know about the nature and character of God. And I listen carefully for God to speak as I sit with Him, mouth shut, Bible open, pen in hand.

The image of these four chairs lingered. Many streams of thought immediately began to flow as the picture of the four chairs solidified in my mind. Most ended up quickly breaking down. But a few main thoughts emerged, the fleshing out of which make up the chapters in this book. My initial pursuit followed this broad thought: "What are the implications of drawing in and taking my place in the fourth chair?" Many questions ignited from there: "Is this metaphor substantial enough to hold up under a long examination? Is it in any way disrespectful to God, somehow making less of Him than He is? When I draw near to Him, am I in fact drawing in to the fullness of who He is? How much have I thought about God, as One being, yet three distinct Persons?" And on and on the questions came.

I process thoughts as thoroughly as I'm able, and very slowly. I'm in no hurry because this is a process I truly love. I imagine myself in some grand old library, sitting at a table, the Lord standing over my shoulder and instructing me. This broad thought percolated for months: "What are the implications of this picture?" I mentally sat and looked at those four empty chairs for days on end, trying to envision each of us sitting there, wondering who sat where and if that mattered at all. I wondered about the casual, even intimate, arrangement of these chairs. I wrestled with the possible irreverence of the scene.

I was conscious that I had never thought about the possibility that being in the presence of God might mean I was in the presence of *all of Him*. Who thinks long and hard about the Trinity, let alone their relationship to Him? The thought of being in proximity to Him, perhaps all of Him at once, was foreign. And then I wondered, "Does it even matter? Am I making too much of nothing, thinking about things too lofty for me? Maybe this was stuff meant for scholars and theologians to wrestle through and then inform the rest of us about.

But then this familiar churning began in my spirit that drives me to press in to the Word of God and pull on His coattail for answers. He gave me a brain, and He has my ear, and He wants to speak—to me. And while He brings me teachers through books and sermons. He has been intent for me to come to terms with this: He means to be my primary Teacher. I lack for nothing but the will to pursue Him and the determination to carve out the space to draw away with Him. I believe He extends that invitation universally to every Child of God, regardless of age, depth of understanding about Spiritual things, status, or the geographic space we occupy on Planet Earth.

I pressed in with this metaphor of the four chairs, applying myself to Paul's admonition to *"test everything; hold fast what is good"* (1 Thess. 5:21). Many times, I had to draw back and remind myself this was simply a mental picture, something God may or may not use to teach me about what it means to be in His presence.

What came into my mind as I thought about being in God's presence? I had for years known Him as an invitational God. Scripture clearly reveals I've been invited to come to Him, even to enter His courts with praise; to come to His throne confidently. It's equally clear that I'm to come with a contrite heart, with respect, aware of His greatness. The paradox of maintaining awe and reverence, even fear of God, while remembering I'm His treasured and welcomed daughter, is a mystery I'm asked to hold. So I practiced holding it as I opened the Scriptures and asked Him to meet with me.

The Bible is rich in metaphors having to do with our proximity to God. So the precedent is there. But of course it's critical to keep clearly in mind the difference between what's literal and what's figurative. A metaphor likens one thing to another but is meant to make its point and no more. Psalm 78 says God led His people like sheep, guiding them in the wilderness like a flock. Isaiah says we, like sheep, have gone astray. Peter reuses that likeness in his letter: *"For you were straying like sheep, but have now returned to the Shepherd and Overseer of your souls"* (1 Peter 2:25).

Jesus frequently used metaphors. He spoke to His beloved friends using a vineyard to make a critical point about their connection to Him and about His connection to The Father. When Jesus spoke in public, He very often offered an image in which to consider the point he wanted to make. When Jesus wept over Jerusalem, He confessed His longing to care for its people, like a hen gathering her chicks.

As the months came and went, I became increasingly confident that I could look at the four chairs and learn and that God would use this image to expand my understanding in critical ways. And I have learned. I've examined the four chairs under the Spirit's watchful eye, as if it were a mock-up, looking at it from every possible angle. In the process, God has reminded me of His altogether otherness, sometimes to caution me, but always to inspire awe within me. He has also reminded me of His altogether approachability, so that while I have learned with Him, I have also experienced Him in the learning. I know Him better. We are closer in relationship with one another.

Having said that, I am acutely aware that any ground gained in my proximity to or experience of God is due to His patient tending of me. I've peered with more clarity at my own personal weakness and shortsightedness. In spite of significant growth in my relationship with God, I have also grappled with my tendency to resist His invitation to keep growing.

He has always stood ready to receive me to Himself, eager for me to come, pointing me to the empty chair in His presence. That it took me as long as it did to gain any ground on that path exposed a fortitude of resistance amassed through my untended childhood wounds and an entrenched determination to be captain of my own ship. How grateful I am that God was far more determined that I experience life in the fullness of how I was designed to experience it! The words of Jesus are true: *"I am the good shepherd. I know My own and My own know Me, just as the Father knows Me and I know the Father; and I lay down My life for the sheep"* (John 10:14–15).

To move toward the fourth chair is to move toward "I *am*," the singular, great, and mighty God, who made all that is, who sustains all life, and who is bound by nothing. The universe He created cannot contain Him. He is altogether other than. Yet He made Himself in the likeness of man, revealing His desire for fellowship and revealing the depths to which He would go to provide it. Love drives Him toward us, but we must humbly walk the narrow path He has illuminated to meet Him. Our legs should weaken a bit as we walk, our hearts beating faster as we draw nearer. We ought to have a mixture of fear and anticipation, knowing in our souls we're approaching the One by whom and for whom we were made.

> *"But God, being rich in mercy, because of the great love with which He loved us, even when we were dead in our trespasses, made us alive together with Christ —by grace you have been saved— and raised us up with Him and seated us with Him in the heavenly places in Christ Jesus, so that in the coming ages He might show the immeasurable riches of His grace in kindness toward us in Christ Jesus. For by grace you have been saved through faith. And this is not your own doing; it is the gift of God, not a result of works, so that no one may boast. For we are His workmanship, created in Christ Jesus for good works, which God prepared beforehand, that we should walk in them."*
> —Ephesians 2:4–11

Chapter 2

Three Chairs for God
Three, Yet One

As I contemplated writing about this metaphor—especially because three of the four chairs are occupied by God the Father, the Son, and the Holy Spirit—I realized how painfully little I understood about the history of the doctrine of the Trinity. I believed it unequivocally, but I had never made it my business to find out for myself how Christianity came to settle on the language that describes God in His oneness and diversity.

On the face of it, it doesn't seem as if it would impact my spiritual journey all that much whether or not I could engage intelligently in a conversation about the persons of the Trinity. As I recall my particular past, I received no substantive teaching from the pulpit about the subject. It's possible I would not have been able to assimilate that teaching even if I had received it. I did not practice the discipline of taking what I heard on a Sunday morning and sitting with the Lord at home with my Bible open so He could help work those truths into me. But I've come to believe strongly that with every bit of truth I am given, a transaction with the Lord must take place, where that truth moves from my system of belief into action. If truth doesn't improve my behavior, it's not yet part of me.

One of the many changes that took place in me, as I drew into the presence of God with the picture of the four chairs in my mind, was a radical and permanent shift in my thoughts and emotions. I'll explore that shift throughout the book, but there was an immediate effect every time I came into the throne room simply because I was conscious of God in a way that more accurately reflected who He is. It didn't matter that I could barely understand that diversity. Simply having the thought that I was moving toward one Being who was in fact three Persons, profoundly altered my countenance as I approached Him. He was far greater, far more diverse, far more mysterious in His otherness than I had ever contemplated before.

I believe that realization caused me to come to Him with a heart attitude that was more befitting the King, even a loving invitational King. I would now say, unhesitatingly, it matters a great deal that I have the basic framework of the doctrine of the Trinity and that I am able to engage with some conviction about the subject. Lest that statement cause you to shrink away, even great theologians come to the edge of what can be understood and embrace (uncomfortably at times) the unfathomable mystery of our Triune God.

We have two thousand years of insight from men and women who have prayerfully opened the Bible in pursuit of trinitarian theology. We glean from them but are responsible for our own Holy Spirit-led exploration of the Scriptures for insight.

I wonder if it would surprise you to know that a high percentage of Christians are not only in the same boat

I was in terms of a lack of knowledge about Trinitarian Theology, but have come to conclusions about the Trinity that are entirely false according to what Christians hold as orthodox. In my research, I came across a news article titled "Survey Finds Most American Christians Are Actually Heretics."[1]

Reporting our lack of understanding about the relationship between Father, Son and Spirit, it kindly referred to us as "accidental blasphemers." Perhaps our lack of understanding reveals a lack of desire to respond to God knocking on the door of our hearts. We have a rich theology to explore in His presence, and we find ourselves deeply and dangerously in the deficit when we do not explore it. Might we be dying of thirst without the awareness that our souls are perilously parched?

A survey conducted in 2014 by Ligonier Ministries and LifeGate Research reported that while the majority of Americans believed God is perfect, the answers revealed that Americans wanted God on their own terms. Some results reflected healthy thinking, but many of the results showed a lack of orthodox thinking about God. This is especially true of questions related to the Trinity. One in five Americans denied that Jesus is the God-man. One-third of Americans thought the Father is more divine than the Son. The member of the Trinity that is the least understood in the United States is the Holy Spirit.[2]

The 2020 version of the same survey revealed that a majority of US adults (59 percent) say the Holy Spirit

---

1. "Survey Finds Most American Christians Are Actually Heretics," G. Shane Morris, *The Federalist*, October 10, 2016, https://thefederalist.com/2016/10/10/survey-finds-american-christians-actually-heretics/.
2. "The State of Theology," Ligonier, October 28, 2014, https://www.effectiveministry.org/wp-content/uploads/2014/12/The-State-Of-Theology-White-paper.pdf.

is a force, not a personal being. The updated survey also reports that not only does the majority of the general US population reject the deity of Christ; now 30 percent of evangelicals agree that He was merely a great teacher and was not God.[3]

These findings reveal a frightening acceleration in the decline of our understanding of Orthodox Christianity. If professing Evangelical Christians don't know what they believe, how can we possibly introduce people to the true Gospel? Even more, can a Christian experience God without knowing the core ways He reveals Himself in the Bible? We pursue the people who mean something to us by moving toward them and finding out who they are. We do that because it is the only path to experiencing true relationship. We shouldn't be surprised by the part we must play in cultivating meaningful relationship with God. Somehow that doesn't seem to be moving most of us in His direction.

God has revealed in His Word enough about Himself, however faintly, for us to grasp one Being, yet three Persons. The Law of Gravity proves a compelling comparison in terms of believing in something we cannot fully explain. Sir Isaac Newton described gravity as a force. Albert Einstein later likened it to the "consequence of the curvature of spacetime." We theorize about the way in which gravity works but acknowledge the irrefutable evidence that gravity exists. We believe in the law of gravity even without the ability to explain it adequately.

The grandeur and mystery of our universe, as well as the laws that are in place to govern it, provide a framework in which to think deeply about the mysteriousness of God,

---

3. "The State of Theology," Ligonier, 2020, https://thestateoftheology.com/.

who created all that exists. Humans have been pondering these thoughts for thousands of years. The psalmist said it this way: *"By the word of the Lord the heavens were made, and by the breath of His mouth all their host. He gathers the waters of the sea as a heap; He puts the deeps in storehouses. Let all the earth fear the Lord; let all the inhabitants of the world stand in awe of Him! For He spoke, and it came to be; He commanded, and it stood firm"* (Ps. 33:6–9).

The Bible speaks to the oneness and diversity of God right from the opening pages. The story of creation tells us God created all that exists. It tells us the Spirit of God was hovering over the waters. It reveals His plurality in the creation of humans (see Genesis 1:26–27). The book of John reveals that Jesus, the Word, was part of the creation act: *"In the beginning was the Word, and the Word was with God, and the Word was God. He was in the beginning with God. All things were made through Him, and without Him was not any thing made that was made" (John 1:1–3).* And Paul's letter to the Colossians says, *"For by Him (Jesus) all things were created, in heaven and on earth…"* (Col. 1:16). The whole of the Trinity was present and active in the act of creation.

R. C. Sproul said in his book *Everyone's a Theologian*, "We cannot conceive of how one being could be contained in three Persons and still be only one being. To that extent, the doctrine of the Trinity in this formulation is mysterious; it boggles the mind to think of a being who is absolutely one in His essence yet three in person."[4]

What is the orthodox view regarding God in three Persons? We can't responsibly move into a conversation

4. R. C. Sproul, *Everyone's a Theologian: An Introduction to Systematic Theology* (Sanford, Florida: Ligonier Ministries, 2019). 58.

about the four chairs without at least a basic trinitarian framework. The Gospel Coalition published an article written by Kevin DeYoung that distills succinctly what trinitarian theology builds on. DeYoung says this:

> The doctrine of the Trinity can be summarized in seven statements. (1) There is only one God. (2) The Father is God. (3) The Son is God. (4) The Holy Spirit is God. (5) The Father is not the Son. (6) The Son is the not the Holy Spirit. (7) The Holy Spirit is not the Father. All of the creedal formulations and theological jargon and philosophical apologetics have to do with safeguarding each one of these statements and doing so without denying any of the other six.[5]

DeYoung cites the Creeds in his article because they provide the earliest statements of faith from theologians in the early church. Here is a thumbnail historical picture of the origin of the Doctrine of the Trinity. The forefathers of our faith, as early as AD 220, articulated the diversity of God by referring to Him as three Persons in one Being. While a version of the word "trinity" is found in the writings of the Greek theologian Theophilus around AD 180, it was the writer Turtullian who gave us the Latin word *Trinitas* to express the idea that God is One Being, yet three Persons—one in unity, three in Persons. So core is this belief that it became and remains a foundational underpin of our Christian doctrine. Theologians have wrestled throughout the centuries seeking

---

5. "The Doctrine of the Trinity: No Christianity Without It," Kevin DeYoung, Gospel Coalition, September 28, 2011, https://www.thegospelcoalition.org/blogs/kevin-deyoung/the-doctrine-of-the-trinity-no-christianity-without-it/

further insight into this great mystery, but the essence of Turtullian's original interpretation of the Scriptures has prevailed.

In AD 325, Emperor Constantine I ordered a council to convene in response to growing heresies that had risen in opposition to Christian beliefs. This ecumenical council of Christian bishops was charged to refute those heresies, which resulted in the original Nicene Creed. A second council convened in AD 381, giving us the rendering still widely adhered to by Christians as our doctrine of faith. Neither this creed, nor any subsequent creed (namely the Apostle's Creed and the Athanasian Creed), is more than a statement of faith based on what the Bible states about God—Father, Son, and Spirit.

Painstakingly, prayerfully chosen language encapsulates what we believe as Christians. These creeds are not meant to serve in place of the Word of God in any way; rather, they serve as a testimony of belief. It provides the earliest insight into the Christian view of the Trinity. The Nicene Creed is worth a careful, prayerful reading. Our Christian forefathers penned it more than sixteen hundred years ago, so it is not only a treasured piece of our church history but a reliable statement of faith for Christians, with particular attention paid to the godhead.

The Nicene Creed—Agreed at the Council of Constantinople, 381

"I believe in one God,
the Father almighty,
maker of heaven and earth,
of all things visible and invisible;
I believe in one Lord Jesus Christ,
the Only Begotten Son of God,

born of the Father before all ages.
God from God, Light from Light,
true God from true God,
begotten, not made, consubstantial with the Father;
through him all things were made.
For us men and for our salvation
He came down from heaven,
and by the Holy Spirit was incarnate of
the Virgin Mary,
and became man.
For our sake he was crucified under
Pontius Pilate,
he suffered death and was buried,
and rose again on the third day
in accordance with the Scriptures.
He ascended to heaven
and is seated at the right hand of the Father.
He will come again in glory
to judge the living and the dead
and his kingdom will have no end.
I believe in the Holy Spirit, the Lord, the giver of life,
who proceeds from the Father [and the Son],
who with the Father and the Son is adored and glorified,
who has spoken through the prophets.
I believe in one, holy, catholic and apostolic Church.
I confess one Baptism for the forgiveness of sins
And I look forward to the resurrection of the dead
and the life of the world to come. Amen."[6]

Isaiah 44:6 says, *"I am the first and I am the last; besides me there is no God."* There is only one God, yet God is three distinct persons. God is one being or essence.

---

6. "Nicene Creed, Christianity," Britannica, https://www.britannica.com/topic/Nicene-Creed.

Each Person is eternal and co-equal. They are complete within themselves, having no need beyond themselves. You will find, as you investigate trinitarian theology, that there are differing views even about the statements I have just made. There are theories about the godhead having a hierarchical ordering—the Father being in some way positionally over the Son and the Spirit. I hold to the lines drawn by our forefathers, who believed the arrangement of Father, Son, and Spirit is egalitarian. They are each equal in status, yet unique to the others in their personhood. The Creeds, specifically the Nicene Creed, the Apostle's Creed, and the Athanasian Creed, each bear this out, emphatically stating that all three entities are eternal, and all are God.

Beyond these statements of faith, there is much we do not and cannot understand. This is simply because we, as finite creatures, are searching for the ability to wrap our minds around what is outside the linear, time-oriented reality we experience.

With this basic trinitarian theology in place, we turn to the metaphor and understand why three of the four chairs represent the three Persons of God. It simply wouldn't do to have a single chair in front of me for three Person's to occupy. Now I have a fixed image in my mind, and I "see" before me Father, Son, and Spirit. I'm aware that I'm connected to each of them; and uniquely so.

Each connection is familial. Each is highly personal and highly relational. I am caught up anew in the wonder of whose company I occupy. And how can I be uniquely related to different aspects of One Being? The Word of God makes it plain.

I am in relationship with God the Father as His child. This was solidified as I received the gift of eternal life (salvation) from Jesus by faith: *"But to all who did receive Him, who believed in His name, He gave the right to become children of God"* (John 1:12). The gift of "sonship" that is mine through faith in Christ comes with full benefits, as if I were His natural-born child. Adoption into God's family means a full grafting in. It is a description of my spiritual birth. It is not earned or merited in any way, yet it comes to me as I receive it by faith.

No earthly relationship between a father and his child is comparable to the quality of love and care I receive from Father God. God writes the book on Fatherhood. He defines it. He lives it out. He proves it generation after generation, age after age. He is the embodiment of goodness and love. He is fiercely protective and loyal. He never breeches trust or fails in any way to provide. He is a perfect Father: *"See what kind of love the Father has given to us, that we should be called children of God; and so we are…"* (1 John 3:1).

It's difficult not to superimpose the experience of our earthly fathers on God the Father. Whatever our story, that kind of application sells God woefully short. That's very good news for all of us, even if we have had wonderful, nurturing earthly fathers. God's fathering ways are meant to influence the way earthly fathers care for their children, but we cannot with integrity hold up any earthly lens as we look at our Heavenly Father. God alone defines and establishes the template for fatherhood.

I am also uniquely in relationship with the second person of the Godhead, God the Son. I relate to Him in many ways, but only because He is first my Savior. The Bible is clear about the fact that a soul is saved from eternal separation from God only by faith in the finished work of Jesus: *"I am the way, and the truth, and the life.*

No one comes to the Father except through Me" (John 14:6).

In Jesus, whom the Bible states is the expressed image of God, I experience all the "languages" of love. He is a nurturing, compassionate God that defines Storge (affection and nurturing). He is the embodiment of *Philos* (Greek for friendship), being a steadfast companion and true friend. He even embodies the purest ideals of *Eros* (the state of "being in love") as the beloved groom who longs to be united with His bride. Each of these gifts of love that I receive from the heart of Jesus is summed up in *Agape* (unconditional service), the unconditional, never-changing love that serves, simply for the sake of serving. It comes without any expectation of reciprocation. Agape, described for us in the beautiful passage from 1 Corinthians 13, is precisely the way I am loved by God, demonstrated through the earthly life of Jesus.

I am also a coheir with Jesus: *"The Spirit Himself bears witness with our spirit that we are fellow heirs with Christ"* (Rom. 8:16). *"Listen, my beloved brothers, has not God chosen those who are poor in the world to be rich in faith and heirs of the kingdom, which He has promised to those who love Him?"* (James 2:5). Jesus and I share in the inheritance of the riches of God. We are joint heirs.

Finally, I am intimately connected to God though relationship with the beloved third Person of the trinity: *"And I will ask the Father, and He will give you another Helper, to be with you forever"* (John 14:16).

I have the gift of the unending presence of the Holy Spirit within me. As such, I become a place of residence for Him: *"Do you not know that you are God's temple and that God's Spirit dwells in you?"* (1 Corin. 3:16). *"Or do you not know that your body is a temple of the Holy Spirit within you, whom you have from God?"* (1 Corin. 6:19).

What are the implications of the literal indwelling of the Holy Spirit for you and me? It's meant to comprehensibly change the way we view ourselves. It's meant to remind us that we are owners of nothing, not even our own bodies. Rather, we steward—our bodies, our gifts, our callings, our possessions, our relationships, and our spheres of influence. God's presence within us guides that stewardship so that we live in cooperation with Him.

Jesus introduced the Spirit as Helper. The breadth of ways He helps is equal to the ways we are in need. He advises, He comforts, He convicts, He intercedes, He reminds, He instructs. He is our chief and indispensable companion.

As men and women of the Word, we owe sole credit to the Holy Spirit for any advancement of spiritual understanding or any increased insight of the Scriptures. The Holy Spirit waits for us to open the Word of God. He means for us to experience the Bible as a living book—not only to teach and keep teaching, but to greatly enhance our experience of Himself. We're meant to know God infinitely better for having spent time with the Holy Spirit in His Word. There is no substitute for this primary inroad to the heart of God.

He also provides an indispensable retrieval service, grabbing relevant truths out of the archives of our memory bank and bringing them to the fore of our minds. If you've ever experienced having just the right truth present at just the right moment, you have benefited from the Spirit's guiding whisper: *"But the Helper... will teach you all things and bring to your remembrance all that I have said to you"* (John 14:26).

The Spirit of God is also responsible for convicting us of wrongdoing—of sin. This gift of conviction is meant to drive us to confession and repentance. While the dissonance we experience is a terrible thing to feel, it is a necessary alert to the presence of sin. Conviction from the Holy Spirit ends up being a great display of God's kindness. It keeps us aligned with Him for our good and for the good of those we influence—all for His glory.

The reality that I am uniquely related to each of the Persons of the godhead, ignited a thought that was new to me: "Are the other two Persons of the Godhead present in me as the Spirit is present?" Look at this carefully, from John 14:18–23: *"I will not leave you as orphans; I will come to you. Yet a little while and the world will see me no more, but you will see me. Because I live, you also will live. In that day you will know that I am in my Father, and you in me, and I in you. If anyone loves me, he will keep my word, and my Father will love him, and we will come to him and make our home with him."*

God has come to me and made His home with me. The fullness of God has come to me. This beautiful, mysterious godhead has captured me for Himself, offering me relationship with the whole of who He is. Desire driven by love is the only explanation for His pursuit of me because God is complete within Himself. He lacks for nothing. He is in need of nothing, yet the Father loves me, as does the Son, as does the Spirit. They love…He loves me.

The Love of God
"Could we with ink the ocean fill
And were the skies of parchment made
Were every stalk on earth a quill
And every man a scribe by trade
To write the love of God above

Would drain the ocean dry
Nor could the scroll contain the whole
Though stretched from sky to sky

O love of God, how rich and pure!
How measureless and strong!
It shall forevermore endure,
The saints' and angels' song."
—A poem written by Frederick M. Lehman in 1917

Chapter 3

Entering the Dialogue
What's Already Going On

It is not a novel thought that God is present and that we can engage Him. Nor is it a novel thought to recognize the existence of God the Father, God the Son, and God the Spirit as three separate Persons. It wasn't until those two thoughts merged that I became keenly aware that I was in fact thinking about a triune being, even as I focused on one of His Persons.

That might seem ridiculous. But for many years as I sought to engage with God, the particulars of the engagement were slightly fuzzy. As I reflect back, I'm pretty sure I was thinking about God as if He were a menu of Persons I could select from. "Who do I want to talk to? Maybe Jesus? Actually, I could really use a talk with the Father." But what if no matter who I was directing my prayer toward, I was, in reality, drawing toward the presence of the fullness of the triune God? Honestly, this was a radical and exciting thought. Also a bit terrifying. As I began to think about this idea, allowing myself to "see" God in three Persons, I asked myself, "What are these three Persons who share an essence doing? Wouldn't they certainly be engaged with each other? Wouldn't they be actively interacting?"

This began to matter a great deal to me because if this were true, then as I drew near the fourth chair, I would likely be entering a community already in dialogue with one another. In other words, I might be entering a conversation already taking place. For me, this was a significant shift in perspective and, generally speaking, a very welcomed one. Once again, the picture of four chairs forced me to think differently in a most unexpected way.

The Persons of the Trinity, a community of three, commune within themselves. Once I allowed that thought to linger in my mind, it was not so difficult to imagine Father, Son and Spirit dialoguing with one another. And why wouldn't they be? They are bound together in one essence, never separated. This was the inroad I followed that shifted my thinking so I could begin to truly see God as a community of three, even if I was focusing my prayers toward one of His Persons.

"Holy Spirit, please give me words of life for my husband today," I might pray. But as I was praying to the Spirit, I was now aware that I was also in the presence of the Father and the Son. How would this shift in perspective change *your* heart as you prayed? I felt a sense of community while I was praying that I had never considered before. My trust in the Lord grew as I contemplated my prayer company having significantly grown in number! My reverence for God grew and my faith deepened because I was more deeply aware of my proximity to God in His fullness.

Did this mean that as I prayed to the Spirit, the Father and Son were listening? Were they attentive to my directed prayer? Did they look knowingly at one another as the Spirit received my words, and were they engaged within themselves as I engaged with the Spirit? Were they dialoguing about how they were going to respond to my prayer? Was Jesus interceding for me before the Father while I prayed? Was the Holy Spirit funneling my words toward the Father, having conformed them so they were in accordance with the Father's will? These weren't necessarily questions I needed answers to. Yet each of these thoughts thoroughly destroyed my previous perceptions about what was happening as I conversed with God. I was now open to a larger story, whether or not I could comprehend it.

I was also wakening more deeply to the paradox of intimacy and reverence with God—*"The friendship of the LORD is for those who fear Him"* (Ps. 25:14). There was no doubt that my sense of reverence grew as I imagined being in the presence of Father, Son and Spirit all at once. The idea that there could also be a growing familiarity akin to friendship was a beautiful thing to consider. Interestingly, as I looked upon the triune God in my mind, I would "see" the marriage of reverence and intimacy they held for each other. That I could also partake in that was an amazing discovery.

Those thoughts gave way to a growing curiosity about what a conversation between the Persons of the trinity might be like. How would they converse? Would there be a dialect or language I might understand if I could witness their interaction? I was struck by the fact that they have been in community from eternity; that they are never changing in their nature; and that whatever I could discover about how they dialogued, it had always been taking place.

We have plenty of evidence in the Bible that the Trinity is fundamentally, essentially an interrelational being. It was starting to make sense to me that God would naturally be very eager for me to know that about Himself, especially in light of the invitation He has extended for me to enter His presence and engage with Him.

The Holy Scriptures offer me a briefing of sorts so that I'm not coming into the presence of God entirely uninformed. Before you meet a dignitary, you are typically briefed so you have some idea of what to expect from him or her, as well as what's expected of you. It's understood that you're entering an unknown situation, and there is protocol in place for the benefit of those in the room. Sprinkled through the Bible are passages giving us a frame of reference for how Father, Son, and Spirit are engaged with one another.

"When Jesus also had been baptized and was praying, the heavens were opened, and the Holy Spirit descended on Him in bodily form, like a dove; and a voice came from heaven, 'You are My beloved Son; with You I am well pleased'" (Luke 3:21–22). God gave a public glimpse of the diversity of Himself in this passage from the Gospel of Luke.

Here, the three Persons of the Trinity were present and engaged with one another. On that day, all those attending the baptism conducted by John the Baptist bore witness to this interaction between Father, Son, and Spirit. Jesus, the Son, was in human form. The Spirit of God took the form of something like a dove and descended on Jesus, and the voice of God the Father was heard from the heavens declaring that He was pleased with His Son. This scene is a treasure of insight into the relational nature of God in three Persons.

Where else in the Bible do we find evidence of the Triune God interacting within Himself? We already know the

Trinity worked cooperatively in the creation of the world and mankind. What else do we know? When God drives Adam and Eve from the garden, He alludes to His plurality: *"Behold, the man has become like one of Us in knowing good and evil…"* (Gen. 3:22). A few chapters later in Genesis, God confuses the language of humanity in response to what the building of the tower of Babel revealed about their hearts: *"Come, let Us go down there and confuse their language"* (Gen. 11:7). And in Isaiah 6:8, God says, *"Whom shall I send, and who will go for Us?…"* These Scriptures speak about God pluralistically, God taking action as an "Us." But the Bible is also generous with passages (like the reference above in Luke 3) that tell us about His Persons being in dialogue with one another.

Jesus comforted His disciples (see John chapters 15 and 16) before His death by revealing the gift that God the Spirit was going to be when He would descend on them at Pentecost. He spent time helping them see the personhood and uniqueness of the Spirit of God. He was introducing them to someone they would come to know very intimately and in a manner almost no one had previously experienced. The presence of God the Spirit would allow them to experience God no less powerfully than when they were with God the Son. The Spirit would essentially represent Jesus, not unlike Jesus essentially represented the Father.

How could these three Persons represent one another without having a cooperative, interactive, and ongoing dialogue with one another? Before Jesus's death, we are privy to one side of a conversation between Jesus and the Father. The High Priestly Prayer found in John chapter 17 gives us a deep and rich look at the intimacy between Father and Son as they speak to one another.

There is a familiarity and ease of speech that Jesus uses: *"All Mine are Yours, and Yours are Mine…"* (verse 10). *"That they may be one, even as We are one"* (verse 11). *"You, Father, are in Me, and I in You, that they also may be in Us, so that the world may believe that You have sent Me. The glory that You have given Me I have given to them, that they may be one even as We are one, I in them and You in me, that they may become perfectly one, so that the world may know that You sent Me and loved them even as You loved Me. Father, I desire that they also, whom You have given Me, may be with Me where I am, to see My glory that You have given Me because You loved Me before the foundation of the world. O righteous Father, even though the world does not know You, I know You, and these know that You have sent Me. I made known to them Your name, and I will continue to make it known, that the love with which You have loved Me may be in them, and I in them"* (verses 20–26).

While Jesus walked the Earth, active, intimate dialogue took place between Father and Son that gives us insight today into a kind of exchange that has been happening from the beginning of time.

We also know from Hebrews chapter 7 that Jesus, who now sits at the right hand of God the Father, makes intercession for us. He's literally conversing with the Father regarding His followers. He's talking to the Father about us and asking for all manner of things on our behalf. I find myself surprised and in awe of that fact, though it should not come as a surprise at all. It stands to reason that His interaction with the Father while He was on the Earth would be reflective of what it has always been.

God the Spirit also goes before the Father on our behalf: *"Likewise the Spirit helps us in our weakness. For we do not know what to pray for as we ought, but the Spirit*

Himself intercedes for us with groanings too deep for words. And He who searches hearts knows what is the mind of the Spirit, because the Spirit intercedes for the saints according to the will of God" (Rom. 8:26–27). It's as if the Holy Spirit takes my prayers and shapes them so that when they come to the ears of the Father, they are in perfect harmony with His will. That's an incomprehensible kind of personal care.

The highly active conversational nature of the Trinity is one of the most inspiring, compelling aspects of who He is. That He is lovingly conversing about His followers astonishes me. Why? Because God is complete within Himself. He is in need of nothing outside Himself. He could understandably confine His dialogue to the beauty and glory of Himself, but He spends at least some of His language on His beloved children. And what He is saying, He says for the advancement of my good so I live life to the fullest. My Triune God means for me to thrive. How does that not radically change the attitude of my heart as I approach the four chairs? It changes everything!

At this point, it's worth emphasizing that the three Persons of the Trinity are entirely and always of one mind and one divine will. Theologians refer to this as "the unity of the Trinity." They never discuss opposing thoughts, plans, or ideas. They never engage in debate, nor do they ever try to put a view forward that might be in conflict with another person of the Trinity. They are of singular mind and singular will. A. W. Tozer, a strong trinitarian, wrote about God as a unitary being—in other words, having no parts. He said, "God has no parts anymore than a diamond has parts. God is all one God, and everything that God does harmonizes with everything else God does. There are no parts to get out of joint and no attributes to face each other and get out of joint. All God's attributes are one and together."[1] So—no arguing, no conflicts to resolve, no pitting one against the other to leverage an idea, no negotiating or stonewalling or buttering up! Just three Divine Persons making their equally vital contributions to whatever they are dialoguing about.

When Jesus took the form of a man, Orthodox Theology refers to Him as then having two wills, one human and one divine (Dyothelitism). But even in His earthly life, we see a perfect display of deference and cooperation. We read about Jesus in the garden of Gethsemane (see Matthew 26:39–44), asking the Father if the "cup" before Him could be removed but submitting His will to the Father's will, His human will to the divine will of God. When Jesus ascended back to the Father, after His death and resurrection, the unity of the wills of the Triune God picked up right where they left off. For eternity, the will of the Father, Son, and Spirit is *one*.

When the picture of the four chairs came to me, I was teaching at a pre-K through twelfth grade in a private Christian school. One of my responsibilities there was to care for the faculty on what we called "in-service days" and "staff retreat days." That was the first group I brought this idea to. On our auditorium stage, I arranged four chairs in a small circle facing inward. And then I began to unpack for them thoughts that were then new to me and still developing as I prayed and studied. We learned and grew together under the title of "Entering the Dialogue," and we pondered what it would mean to take our place in the fourth chair. I opened the Bible to passages I've

---

1. A. W. Tozer, *The Attributes of God Volume 1: A Journey into the Father's Heart* (Camp Hill, Pennsylvania: WingSpread Publishers, 2007), 64–65.

just referenced in this chapter, and my colleagues and I prayerfully studied. The metaphor itself provided a profound shift for many of us, changing permanently the way we envisioned God as we drew near Him.

It caused us to ponder some of the mysteries of our great and immeasurable God. We leapt into that "playground" with a God so big, so vast, so incomprehensible, yet so highly relational and invitational. It was as exciting as it was humbling. *"He leads the humble in what is right, and teaches the humble His way"* (Ps. 25:9).

We marveled at God's diversity yet perfect unity within Himself. We were overwhelmed as much by His otherness as we were that we somehow bore His image. The four chairs became a permanent fixture for many of us as we approached God in prayer, and it changed the way we thought about Him as we drew near. It affected our attitudes in the best sense. It changed us, giving us what we believed was a vantage point far more accurate than we had ever had before. It elevated God yet brought Him nearer than ever before. How could it not?

One staff member told me that when she walked into her kitchen after she was introduced to this concept, she was overwhelmed by the reality that God was present with her, noticing the four chairs around her breakfast table (so rudimentary and simple). But for her, that morning and every subsequent morning, she was oriented to what had been true all along. Her eyes were opened to the treasure that is the presence of God with her. That first morning, with her early-morning cup of tea, she drew into one of those chairs and basked in the presence of God—Father, Son, and Spirit, marveling at the gift of His presence.

I look back to the four chairs with the assurance that God is actually three Persons sharing one essence, knowing that when I approach Him, I may in fact be approaching the whole of who He is. When I pray, I might pray to God the Father, by the power of God the Spirit, and in the name of God the Son. Often I speak directly to Jesus, who is my friend and Savior. And there are times when I speak directly to the Spirit of God, who indwells me. But whomever my prayer might be directed toward, God is there—the fulness of God is there.

It has literally changed my life, practicing the discipline of remembering that God is communing within Himself as I draw near. Equally influencing is the awareness of His altogether otherness. These truths must influence the attitude with which I approach Him. Nothing I know of human interaction can prepare me for what is taking place within the Trinity as I enter His presence.

I "see" the four chairs in my mind. I have gazed at them for several years now. They are never literally occupied as I look at them, but I am always immediately oriented to the meaning. I remember that while it's an absurdity to think Father, Son, and Spirit could actually sit in three chairs, I never want to move toward God without the awareness that I'm moving toward three Persons in active community. I used to imagine approaching God one on One, picturing Him quietly waiting for me to come.

Interestingly, I would nearly always assume the job of initiating conversation. I wonder now that it never occurred to me that He might, having drawn me to Himself, be inviting me to enter a conversation already taking place. I no longer sit across from an empty chair, which I used to do to remind me of His presence with me. That has become too confining. I now see in my mind four chairs, and I slip into the fourth chair to practice the presence of my Triune God, marveling that He has invited me to Himself; into the middle of the mystery of His communion.

> *"The Persons of the Godhead never work sepa-rately. We dare not think of them in such a way as to "divide the substance." Every act of God is done by all three Persons. God is never anywhere present in one Person without the other two. He cannot divide Himself."[2]*
> —A. W. Tozer

---

2. A. W. Tozer, *Tozer on the Holy Spirit: A 365-Day Devotional* (Chicago: The Moody Bible Institute of Chicago, 2020), devotional for January 12.

Chapter 4

Anything but Arbitrary
Called by Name

"I have called you by name…"
—Isaiah 43:1

I did session-work as a studio singer for many years. I'd go in to a studio and typically be one of several singers providing background vocals for people's recording projects. Sometimes, I would get hired simply to fill a needed part, and other times, I was specifically requested. In other words, "Hire a reliable soprano." Or, "Can you call Anne Barbour for this session?" There's nothing personal about being a hired soprano. There would always be a long line of eager and talented women waiting for those coveted calls. If you got the call, and especially if you wanted to get called again, you would make sure you did an A+ job, drawing just enough, but not too much, attention to yourself. You hoped the person who hired you liked you enough to hire you again. It was a highly competitive field.

On the other hand, there was great job security and a highly personal aspect to being specifically requested. It meant there was something inherently unique about my singing voice that the producer was interested in capturing. As long as I showed up and applied myself to what I was uniquely able to do, the person in charge would be pleased and I would get to go home with a paycheck and often a sense of deep satisfaction.

As I consider that the Triune God has extended an invitation to me to draw near to him, I am struck by the nature of His invitation. One of the most significant revelations as I've pondered the picture of the four chairs was this: there is *nothing* arbitrary about His invitation for me to come to Him. There is not simply a place in the presence of God for one of His children to occupy, so that as long as there is an occupant, the position is satisfactorily filled. God does not call nameless sons and daughters to Himself. He does not entreat The Church to draw near. He asks individuals who collectively make up The Church, who have names and personalities and histories and habits and struggles and strengths. That the whole of humanity would come to Him through Christ is His heart's desire. But He knows the names of His children, and we cannot miss the point that while the invitation to enjoy fellowship with God is offered to all who believe, it comes one soul at a time. It's critical that as we think about coming into His presence, we don't see ourselves as having slipped into anonymity in a sea of fellow believers. We are seen and known and invited to move toward Him as the unique individuals we are.

Why would something so simple to understand come as a revelation to me, and so many years after I came to faith? There are contributing factors that reach back as far as the fall of mankind, and forward all the way to the present day. They can be somewhat understood in the framework of what physiologists label Nurture vs. Nature; Genes vs. Environment. I can't minimize the reality of how much my thinking can be shaped by my particular tendencies in combination with a value system shaped and enforced by society and culture, both Christian and non-Christian. Here are but a small handful of examples to help make the point.

In 1913, the United States shifted collectively in the way the work-force operated when Henry Ford introduced the assembly line to make his Model T cars. He borrowed the idea from the cattle industry, which used conveyer belts to move beef through their slaughter houses. As revolutionary as the assembly line was, vastly increasing efficiency and productivity, we began to lose a sense of the value of our individual contribution to an effort.

It's very difficult to maintain that sense of individuality when you become absorbed in a long line of people who are performing rote tasks. We can easily forget that we possess any unique value. In fact, in situations like that assembly line, there is little, if any, place for a person's uniqueness to come to bear. The point is for you to perform your specific task quickly and correctly. The station a person tended was the thing of highest value. Automation would be a major contributor to the reordering of how our culture assigned value to its workers.

In another realm altogether, the arena of compulsory education began to take its current form throughout the nineteenth and twentieth centuries. It was structured to fit the common denominators in students' learning styles, placing those more unique kids who don't fit the education model out on or near the periphery. That environment caused many to struggle significantly—not because they were incapable of learning, but because their learning style was not supported by the methods in place.

We understand this sort of synthesis on a whole new level in the present technologically driven age. Amazon Prime has revolutionized the way we shop so that we now refer to individual establishments as "brick-and-mortar" shops. Once upon a time, the only way you could conduct commerce was in a single-owner establishment. Now, of course, the charm of a "boutique" has more sentimental than remunerative value for the wares it sells. We still like to frequent those kinds of places when we're on vacation because they provide us with a meaningful memory. Amazon hasn't found a way to do that...yet.

A heavy contributor to loss of personal value/identity is that of the invention and implementation of social media. For the first time in history, we have created a venue so accessible you can be "friends" with multiple thousands of people and remain effectively invisible. You can now have "friends" without being known. Arguably, no single invention has moved the global populous closer together while simultaneously disjoining it.

As I write this, the planet is engulfed in a global pandemic. Every country in every continent has altered its normal course of function. Rarely in history does a single event cause such an immediate planetary ripple. Such an event takes the isolation variable formed by social media and pushes it exponentially outward.

In general terms, for a solid one-hundred-years plus, our culture (including our Christian culture) has sought to grow in productivity and efficiency. In doing so, we have forgotten to protect the means by which individuals can make their unique contributions to society. Perhaps we felt it was far too time consuming and expensive. The bottom line is this: there is an inherent danger of dehumanization any time we seek to find uniform ways to do a thing for the sake of increased productivity or accessibility.

I am far more influenced than I know by the value system of my culture and society. Even if I stand in opposition to pieces of that system, the general mindset still colors the ways I think about most veins of life. Without doubt, it had crept into the way I was thinking about God and my relationship to Him. I viewed myself too much as one of a great collective of sons and daughters, blending in as if we melded together to make one giant, colorless blob. I'd misplaced my sense of individuality, and I was applying that to how I viewed God's invitation to draw near to Him. It has and remains a matter of prayer, that God would untangle, detach, or undo any beliefs I hold that keep me from seeing His invitation to me as the shockingly wondrous and highly personal thing that it is.

My precious brothers and sisters, you were formed by God. You are each uniquely reflective of Him. You bear an aspect of His image that no other person who has or ever will live bears. Therefore, anything, or anyone, or any idea or experience that aids in your inability to see clearly; any adversarial voice, or false pronouncement over you; any distraction whatsoever from that view needs to be seen as the potentially diabolical thing that it is. Your enemy delights in your anonymity. He is thoroughly satisfied that you might consider yourself as "Person #37 on conveyor belt #14, in warehouse #8 of the north wing, on the east campus of the giant factory of God." That you would view yourself as such is a huge victory for him and a tragedy for the Kingdom of God.

> *"Thus says the Lord He who created you, O Jacob He who formed you, O Israel: 'Fear not, for I have redeemed you; I have called you by name; you are Mine.'...bring My sons from afar, and My daughters from the end of the earth, everyone who is called by My name, whom I created for My glory, whom I formed and made."*
> —Isaiah 43:1:6–7

I am at once called by God by name—and called by His name. The settling of that reality blew up the idea that the fourth chair could be filled arbitrarily. One of those four chairs was my chair. It was mine, which meant it wasn't anyone else's—which meant what? How often in my journey with God had I abdicated my place in His presence? What were the reasons I used to stay away? I'm sure I most often simply altogether ignored the prompting of God to come to Him.

I also know that on a subconscious level, I used to think those people who were the "deepest" in their faith (whatever I thought that meant) were certainly "with Him" and that He would be happy to have them; therefore, He wouldn't notice if I stayed away. I'm laughing at myself as I write this, but there you go. Maybe you identify! I dismissed. I ignored. I deflected. I downplayed the notion that it mattered one iota if I showed up. How *could* it matter? Seriously, how on Earth could it matter in the least? I knew I needed Him. I knew I was utterly lost without Him. But I did not consider that my presence with Him could impact Him in any measurable way; therefore, how could it matter if I took my place in His presence? He doesn't need anything, after all.

I stared at the picture of the four chairs for months that turned into years, "seeing" my chair, letting God speak to my spirit. I looked until I knew, beyond doubt, that chair was mine to occupy. And the biggest revelation by far was that if I did not occupy it, it would remain empty. Once I wrapped my brain around *that*, I began to understand that it mattered a great deal what I did with this invitation. I wasn't sure why it mattered, but it settled in me…I needed to be there. I actually *had* to be there.

Two simple trains of thought followed. What are the implications for me if I leave my chair empty? And what are they if I take my place in His presence?

The story that comes to mind regarding each of those tracks is found in the book of Exodus. God had extricated the nation of Israel from the land of Egypt after four-hundred years of enslavement to them. God heard the cries of His people and sent a man in to be His instrument for deliverance. This was the first time in this young nation's history that its people were going to get to know the God who had formed them and made them for His glory. They began to see His power and His supremacy. They watched Him warn Pharaoh, letting him know specifically what would happen if he did not let Israel go free, and they saw Him deliver on those threats. In dealing with Egypt, God was giving His chosen ones a look at part of His nature and character.

After the exodus, they found themselves traveling toward a land promised to Abraham, the father of their nation. They were embarking on a budding relationship with God as free people. During this time, God was giving instructions directly to the people to let them know what would be required of them to be the nation He intended them to be. The manner in which God delivered these commandments caused the people to become extremely afraid. Here was God speaking to them, while thunder, flashes of lightening, the sound of trumpets, and smoke billowing from Mount Sinai provided dramatic special effects.

This proved too much for the people. Trembling with fear, they literally, collectively moved away from God's presence. They told Moses that henceforth they wanted indirect communication with God (that seemed to work well enough through the duration of the plagues). Moses could deliver God's words to them because they had in mind they would die if they interacted directly with Him. I wonder if the images of God's wrath against the Egyptians triggered their reaction. Whatever the case, that initited a massive and permanent shift in the relationship because God honored their request for a mediator. Selah.

From that time on, God and Israel would be known for having a contentious relationship. God often referred to His Chosen Ones as obstinate and stiff-necked (He was right), and the Israelites were frequently furious with God for the way in which He guided them (they were insufferably shortsighted and impatient). But I have deep empathy for God's Chosen People. I wasn't given a middle name, but I could easily be called Anne Israel Barbour. They are my kin for certain.

In any case, later on in Israel's history, her people would ask for a king to rule them so they could be like other nations. This further widened the relational gap between God and His chosen people. It's hard to have a relationship with your Maker if you won't go near Him. It's harder still if you come out from under His rulership. They would subjugate themselves to earthly kings, banking on the idea that those kings would remain faithful to God. Of course they came to discover that many of those kings ruled in opposition to God, and the populace suffered greatly for it.

The Israelites dismissed the privilege of speaking directly with God and relinquished the honor of being directly under His Kingship. They faced the same dilemma back then that we face today: How do we sift through two entirely opposing value systems while tempering our innate desire to rule our own lives? What do we do to ensure we will be content to align ourselves with the ways of God?

> *"I was ready to be sought by those who did not ask for Me; I was ready to be found by those who did not seek Me. I said, 'Here I am, here I am,' to a nation that did not call upon My name. I spread out My hands all the day to a rebellious people, who walk in a way that is not good, following their own devices; a people who provoke Me to my face continually…"*
> —Isaiah 65:1–3

What if the Israelites had actually asked God to help them deal with their frustration, as well as the terrible fear they were experiencing? What if they had confessed their desire for an earthly king and the lure they felt seeing other kingdoms who had rulers living among them in the flesh? What might have happened if they had pressed in and allowed themselves the opportunity to cultivate a relationship directly with their God? He was clearly offering it.

These are not easy questions, but they are important ones to contemplate as we consider our own invitation to occupy our place in God's presence. The people of Israel never explored what was possible if only they had drawn near to God and remained there. If they had, perhaps they would have come to know Him as Moses did because God *"used to speak to Moses face to face, as a man speaks to his friend"* (Ex. 33:11). That kind of intimacy doesn't blossom without both parties intentionally pursuing one another and being willing to cultivate a meaningful relationship through honesty, truthfulness, and trust.

In Moses's initial meeting with God, he managed to be both afraid and argumentative. He actually aroused God's anger against him by contending with just about every point of the plan God was laying out before him. It was quite a lengthy conversation, and it always makes me laugh as I read it. Moses really did interject his "concerns," apparently determined to enlighten God to the flaws in the details of His plan. I wonder if Moses came out from hiding, *"for he was afraid to look at God,"* or simply started arguing with his face still hidden away for fear! God was amazingly conciliatory even while *"the anger of Lord was kindled against Moses"* (Ex. 4:14). Don't you find it wondrously hopeful that God had space for Moses's questions, and even his presumptive behavior? I sure do. Stories like that have made me bolder in my dialogue with God—not so I can argue for the sake of arguing, but because I know He makes room for me to work through my initial confusion, frustration, and especially fear.

How does God feel about His Children even in light of their obstinance and disregard? God said this through the prophet Jeremiah: *"I have loved you with an everlasting love; therefore I have continued my faithfulness to you... Is Ephraim* [Jacob's grandson for whom one of the twelve Tribe was named] *my dear son? Is he my darling child? For as often as I speak against him, I do remember him still. Therefore my heart yearns for him; I will surely have mercy on him, declares the LORD"* (Jere. 31:3,20).

Who do you know whose love and devotion is such that they, even in the face of blatant disregard, would yearn for a relationship with their betrayer? When God's heart is set on a person, it remains steadfast. God loves those He makes. We understand love as an intangible concept that grows through trial and error—and hopefully, "chemistry." But God has known and loved me from before the creation of all things, let alone before I was born.

"For You formed my inward parts;
You knitted me together in my mother's womb.
I praise You, for I am fearfully and wonderfully made.
Wonderful are Your works;
my soul knows it very well.
My frame was not hidden from You,
when I was being made in secret,
intricately woven in the depths of the earth.
Your eyes saw my unformed substance;
in Your book were written, every one of them,
the days that were formed for me,
when as yet there was none of them."
—Psalm 139:13–16

God has never intended to love me from afar, but to express His love to me personally. That is His nature. That is the way He loves within Himself as Father, Son, and Spirit. Jesus gave language to the ultimate expression of love with these words: *"Greater love has no one than this, that someone lay down his life for his friends"* (John

15:13). And read these incomprehensible words, meant to pierce our hearts: *"For one will scarcely die for a righteous person—though perhaps for a good person one would dare even to die—but God shows His love for us in that while we were still sinners, Christ died for us"* (Rom. 5:7–8). Died why? To build a bridge to Himself that we could cross by faith. As C. S. Lewis wrote, "He died not for men, but for each man. If each man had been the only man made, He would have done no less."[1]

God has been offering deliverance from death, one human at a time, from the beginning of time. He has also exposed His heart, offering fellowship, even the truest friendship to each individual who calls Him Lord. There is nothing remotely arbitrary about it. He has chosen to put Himself in the position to either be rejected or embraced by me and by you. He has revealed that He is able to feel the pain of that rejection as well as the delight of my embrace. He has proven the unquenchable nature of His love so that as long as I draw breath, He stands ready to receive me—my invitation remains open. Yours does as well.

My young life was dismantled and then rebuilt by God so that I now know, without doubt, He is real. The metaphor of the four chairs was plausible from the beginning. God knew it would capture my imagination the moment it came into my mind. I never had to wrestle through whether or not I believed that God was offering an experience of His presence. How it all might work was another matter.

The thoughts that ensued as I wakened to three of those chairs being occupied by God was and remains one of

---

1. C. S. Lewis, *Perelandra* (United Kingdom: The Bodley Head, 1943).

the most compelling mysteries in life. There He is, Three glorious Persons sharing one essence, each of whom I am uniquely related to, each of whom I know and fellowship with. Each are God, equal in God-ship. Each is eternal and of one mind and heart. Each interjects into the plans they all make, even in the design and creation of all that exists. Each reflects the others and each holds within them the fullness of holiness, love, justice, compassion, grace, purity, power, mercy, and a host of other attributes. Of course these are not descriptions of God as much as they are part of His essence. And how, if they are part of God's essence, could they not be equally present in each of the members of the Trinity? They are adjectives as we observe them in ourselves, but they are nouns as we apply them to God. I might have compassion, but God *is* compassion.

The Trinity has set the bar for healthy, thoroughly satisfying community. It is rich and reciprocal. Perfect servitude and deference is practiced within the Trinity. Each has very person-specific roles to play, and each plays them, never infringing on the Others. Their interaction is the embodiment of harmony. There is no jealousy, one-upmanship, or hierarchical battles. There is however, boundless, unconditional love between them. They joyfully make and receive their unique contributions to one another. They dialogue with one another, and they are happy for me to peek into the inner sanctum as they record for me stories throughout history of pieces of their conversations. Our God is a communal, relational God.

But wonder of all wonders, a reality that I can barely grasp for the way in which it undermines my rational "equilibrium," God has pulled a fourth chair into His company of Three. It is a chair that, by virtue of my life given over to Him through faith in Christ, belongs only to me. As I am engraved on the palm of His hand, so my name is engraved on my invitation to draw near: to reason with Him, to rest in Him, to sup with Him, to abide with Him, to walk with Him.

I have chosen to embrace His invitation to me, and I practice occupying the fourth chair—*my* chair. I sit within His company and enjoy the sweetness of the fellowship of Father, Son, and Spirit. Every moment I linger in His presence, I know Him better. Every moment I practice His presence, I orient rightly to whatever moment in life I find myself. When I leave my chair, which I still sometimes do, I feel the absence of fellowship, and I know He does, too. It matters to Him (it matters to me, too) that I am there and that I remain.

> *"God does not stop at rescuing us;*
> *the purpose of that rescue*
> *is to enjoy fellowship with us."*
> —A. W. Tozer

Part 2

Exposure to God
Finite Meets Infinite

"The man and his wife hid themselves from the presence of the LORD God.
—Adam and Eve in the Garden of Eden, Genesis 3:8

"You cannot see My face, for man shall not see Me and live."
—God speaking to Moses, Exodus 33:20

[Isaiah, upon seeing the Lord] *"…and I said: 'Woe is me! For I am lost!…'"*
—The prophet Isaiah, Isaiah 6:5

"Such was the appearance of the likeness Of the glory of the LORD. And when I saw it, I fell on my face."
—The prophet Ezekiel, Ezekiel 1:28

"Now as he went on his way, he approached Damascus, and suddenly a light from heaven shone around him. And falling to the ground,

*he heard a voice saying to him, 'Saul, Saul, why
are you persecuting Me?' The men who were
traveling with him stood speechless, hearing
the voice but seeing no one. Saul rose from the
ground, and although his eyes were opened, he
saw nothing. And for three days he was without
sight, and neither ate nor drank."*
—Saul on the Damascus Road, Acts 9:3–9

*"When I saw Him, I fell at His feet as though
dead."*
—The apostle John on Patmos, Revelation 1:17

There is some kind of cosmic crash when a finite being comes in proximity to the Great I Am. I'm not sure there is language that can adequately describe such encounters. The souls who met God in the dramatic manner described in the passages above fell to the ground as though they were dead (and likely hoped they were). This, of course, is not the only way God introduced Himself to people through the ages. But when we "see" God in His glory, when He shows Himself to us as the altogether-other being that He is, it rightly leaves an indelible imprint on us (perhaps the understatement of all time).

What happens when finite meets Infinite, when darkness is exposed to Light, when sin is exposed to Holiness? It's the unavoidable paradoxes of that exposure that force us to shift our posture both outwardly and inwardly, both in our behavior and our thinking. Encountering God forces change. You either have to retreat further from Him, move closer to Him, or maybe bury your head. But you can't do *nothing!* We have only to look at God, as the men and women in these passages did, to know and feel the immeasurable discrepancy between ourselves and Him. These men and women didn't need a mirror to learn what they learned. They needed to look at "The King, the Lord of hosts." Nothing stays the same once we "see" God. His very presence alters everything and everyone within the space He occupies.

There is a scene in the first installment of *The Lord of the Rings* trilogy in which Bilbo Baggins is about to embark on his final journey away from Bag End. He is in his home with his trusted friend and advisor, Gandalf the Grey, a very powerful wizard. Gandalf is advising Bilbo to leave behind the Ring of Power before he leaves. His nephew, Frodo, would be its new keeper.

But this powerful Ring had bewitched Bilbo so that he was struggling to give it up. Gandalf had been gently persuading Bilbo to let it go until Bilbo became angry and combative. He had come face to face with the depth of his attachment to the Ring. Gandalf, ultimately in an act of great kindness, rises up in front of Bilbo, showing him a glimpse of his supernatural, other-worldly, and powerful self. Bilbo is understandably terrified. Then Gandalf says this to him: "Bilbo Baggins! Do not take me for a cheap conjurer of tricks! I'm not trying to rob you!" And then he becomes his winsome self again and tenderly says, "I'm trying to help you." Bilbo runs to the safety of his friend Gandalf's arms and cries, the spell of the Ring having been broken. Moments later, Bilbo leaves both the Ring of Power and Bag End, but not before struggling once more to literally open his hand to release the Ring. It had been his idol for so many years.

The great writer Tolkien understood something about our finite nature and our struggle to loosen our grip on those things we are convinced we cannot live without. He understood the great deception that could compel us to go to our death before we would release the very things pulling us to the depths of destruction. Our invitation from God to come and occupy our place in His presence is no less than a call to come and truly live life to the fullest. But our occupancy will require the release of things that will "not go gentle into that good night," to quote the poem by Dylan Thomas.

I came to find that I had collected a few of my own Rings of Power throughout my Christian life. And I wondered why I couldn't keep them safely in my pocket *and* slip into my fourth chair. I believed I could have one hand clutching the rings and the other over my heart, pledging allegiance to both myself and God. He dealt with me in His gentle and tender way, and when necessary, He showed me His "otherness" to waken me from my slumber and rescue me. He will do the same for you if you desire it.

> *"In our abandonment*
> *we give ourselves over to God*
> *just as God gave Himself for us,*
> *without any calculations.*
> *The consequences of abandonment*
> *never enter into our outlook*
> *because our life is taken up in Him."*
> —Oswald Chambers, *My Utmost for His Highest*

Chapter 5

My Greatest Fear
Fully Known, Fully Exposed

"The Lord knows those who are His."
—2 Timothy 2:19

*"No creature is hidden from His sight, but all
are naked and exposed to the eyes of Him to
whom we must give account."*
—Hebrews 4:13

Most people walking the planet have degrees of guardedness with other people. Some are not terribly interested in having another person know them intimately. Other folks are no less than desperate to be known altogether. Some of us can't bear to be transparent at all, and some peg the TMI meter after "Hello." Some of us are shy or introverted and prefer to keep our personal lives to ourselves. Others want anonymity because we have something to hide. And sometimes, we don't want to hide as much as we simply want to mind our own business and have others do the same. Some of us, damaged by past relationships, become either reclusive or overly needy. Some will only be pursued in a relationship, while others must be the initiators. Most often, the bulk of us can be found somewhere on the spectrum between the extremes.

You and I have our own unique behavioral profile. The people who know us best probably have the most accurate view of what that is. Often it's hard for us to honestly see our particular "preferences" about the way we like to have our relationships play out. But if we want to have healthy ongoing interaction with others, sooner or later we have to take a good, long look at the expectations we carry with us.

Buried beneath the nuances of our specific relationship methodology, all of humanity has in common one singular innate longing. We all long to be fully known and loved for who we are. *That* longing is built intentionally into our core, and while it might derive from our emotions, it affects us holistically. God put it there, having every intention of being the One to satisfy it. The design is such that no other will suffice, so that if you don't open up that space for God to enter, you will remain essentially relationally empty. It's a little like pitching a tent and believing it's your dream house. Thus the pursuits of humans from the beginning of time, who strive to find the One to enter that soul space and set up camp.

When one human interacts with another human, there are always two imperfect stories that come together. Those imperfect stories merge and naturally influence the interaction. That's obviously *not* what's happening as I come to meet with God. I couldn't possibly have any personal frame of reference for the convergence of relationship between myself and Almighty God. But I *think* I do because I subconsciously bring my relational rules and preferences with me as I move toward Him.

Just this morning, fighting through the ugly emotional undulations of menopause, I found myself hesitating to pray and sit quietly with the Lord. My heart had been unsettled. My temper had gotten the better of me as I was doing my normal morning routine. I felt weak and shallow emotionally, and I didn't want to bring that into our company. I felt badly about my morning "failures" and succumbed to the voice in my head that said, "You really don't want to 'slime' Jesus with your disagreeable countenance. You're not fit right now. Get yourself together, and *then* engage with Him."

That thinking makes sense only if I'm headed toward another human being, who may, in fact, *not* need to be exposed to the residue of my volatile self. That's a silly illustration, but my point is simply this: the relationship I have with God is unique to any human relationship I will ever have. Therefore, my approach to that relationship is equally unique.

There is no way God would expect me to know instinctively what the differences are between relating to people and relating to God, or even how to navigate them. He has and continues to teach me, and He's happy to do so. It's a class I'm enrolled in for life, which begins the moment I occupy my place in His company.

Maybe it would be easier to think more accurately about communing with God if I had language reserved specifically for that relationship. Alas, I have to do the work of rightly applying the limited relationship language I *do* have to the most significant Person in my life. I cannot think the same, even if I am left to use the same language. My communion with God will have an entirely different quality than anything else I experience with any other person. How could it not?

There are several unique aspects that can make occupying my place in the presence of God a daunting, even frightening proposition. I believe all of us grapple with them from time to time. The first is this: in His company, I am thoroughly known. I'm afraid we might understandably read on too quickly, but that would be a mistake. Is it possible to slow down and hear this with fresh ears? In His company, I am *thoroughly* known. Depending on the various elements of my life at any given moment, that can be as comforting as it may be horrifying.

The reality that God knows me altogether, completely, thoroughly, that there is no single thing about me that He does not fully know, has at times caused me to tremble because as well as I might be known by the people in my life, none of them knows me as God does. Truth has informed my emotions and thoughts every single time I draw near to God. It means I'm drawing near someone who is literally "acquainted with all my ways." If I'm honest, there are times I have chosen *not* to draw near to Him, precisely because I am aware that He *knows* me. I have had to come to terms with my personal desire for a modicum of anonymity even with God, and I struggle when I'm not willing to set that aside. There is no anonymity in the presence of God.

The second reality is cousin to the first: not only am I fully known by God; I am fully exposed. I might hope that while God knows me altogether, I could at least come to Him covered up in some way. But in the company of God, nothing is hidden. The writer of Hebrews was not trying to scare anyone when he wrote that *"all are naked and exposed to the eyes of Him to whom we must give account"* (Hebr. 4:13).

He was stating a fact. That statement is accurate whether or not I'm in God's presence. But when I choose to commune with Him, I do so with my body, mind, emotions, and spirit exposed. The scales are not balanced as I sit in the company of God. My natural self cannot help but wrestle with feeling this is grossly unfair. But my spirit won't waste the energy, aware that it can be no other way, nor should it be.

That exposure, and whatever thoughts or emotions it conjures up, is always a gift. Light exposes what is actually present. Darkness hides it. Shadows distort it. Only when light illuminates, and what's real is revealed, can a thing be seen and addressed. And clearly that's why my natural self can and often does hate the thought of exposure. I say "natural self" because when I'm grumbling about exposure, I'm not operating as the new creation in Christ that I am. The "old man" is striving to resurrect itself in protest.

My friend told me a story of having to address several students who had managed to get themselves into some kind of collective trouble. She, as Dean of Students, was tasked with dealing with those students and informing their parents. The students initially thought they had some leverage over her, assuming only they were in possession of the facts. That assumption vanished as she stated back to them not only what had happened, but who was responsible for it. They would have entered her office very differently had they understood their deeds were exposed before they ever arrived.

Decades ago, a friend and colleague called me to his office to tell me he'd found out that I had not kept his confidence about a matter. That exposure was extremely

The Fourth Chair

74

painful, but so necessary. My transgression was twofold because after my initial transgression, I did not offer my own exposure; he had to confront me about it. I was devastated to have disappointed him. There is nothing so horrible as being found out, knowing you ought to have been the one to go and make your own confession.

But I don't chafe against exposure only as it reveals sin in my life. I can also resist the idea of finding out something's amiss because it's going to impact the flow of my life. Many times, I've put off going to the dentist or the doctor *only* because I didn't want to find out something was wrong. I've hesitated to return phone calls when I knew I was going to talk to someone who might have bad news. I've put off being the bearer of bad news, too. I can be straight up selfish, reluctant to approach people or situations that I know might be messy. After all these years of knowing better, within my natural self remains the erroneous, destructive belief that ignorance is bliss! I have to leave that at the door every time I enter into communion with God.

The truth is, ignorance (lack of exposure to what's true) can be terribly destructive. I am reminded of the Israelites' attack on Ai (see Joshua chapter 8). Two terrible things took place that caused them to be handily routed when it looked as though they should have breezed to victory. The first is, Joshua, their leader, did not draw near to God and seek His counsel as to whether they should attack in the first place. They were fresh off their first and triumphant victory at Jericho. Ai was smaller in population and strength. So they downsized their troops accordingly and charged in.

And here is the second gross error they discovered as Joshua was dialoguing with God *after* the fact: apparently, they were in no way fit to engage the enemy (Who knew!). Joshua had no idea (because he didn't ask) that one of his men had sinned by directly disobeying God's specific instructions about what was to be destroyed and what was to be recovered after the battle of Jericho. They were to keep themselves away from all that was *"devoted to the Lord for destruction"* (Josh. 6:17). So God exposed Achan's sin as well as Joshua's error in not seeking God's counsel. Once all was "seen" and corrected, God sent Israel's armies back in to conquer Ai.

Exposure can be extremely difficult to deal with, but I would be more successful going about my life with my hands over my ears and blindfolded than I would be to resist the ultimate gift that exposure can be. I cannot maneuver through my life without light, therefore exposure. It's a fixed principle that's never smart to resist.

The next thing that is entirely different about relationship with God is a second cousin to the nature of exposure. God knows far more about me than I know about myself. While this is painfully obvious, I often pass over it precisely for that reason. I am almost never face to face with another human being who knows me better than I know myself. I say "almost never" because there are aspects of myself that people who are close to me can see with more clarity than I do—sometimes far more clearly.

Clearly, I come short of knowing everything about myself. I'm discovering, all the time, things hidden in my subconscious—preferences and expectations I didn't even know I had. For instance, when my husband, John, would take me to dinner, I might not think I care which restaurant we would choose. He might ask, "Where would you like to eat tonight?"

I'd answer, "I don't care. Wherever you think."

He'd carefully ask a second time, in case I wasn't sure. I might insist I didn't have an opinion (I would mean it sincerely). Then he would pull into the *"wrong"* restaurant! Oops! Honestly, if in that moment he again asked me, "Where would you like to have dinner?" I'd most likely say, "I don't know. Just not here."

Back when John and I were first dating, I broke off our relationship to pursue my fledgling music "career." I did not ask the Lord if I should do this or not. I felt unable to give myself fully to a new relationship *and* a big career move. Not even twenty-four hours later, I found myself in a panic, certain I had done the wrong thing. I was so young and unaware of myself. Only when I'd make a foolish sweeping adjustment, like breaking up with the man I loved, would the mental lights come on for me.

When I occupy the fourth chair, I'm with Someone who knows me infinitely more than I know myself. I sometimes reimagine those scenes, only now I ask the Lord for guidance. He would have given it willingly back then, if only I had asked Him.

The comforting feeling I have when I remember God's comprehensive knowledge of me can also been a source of trepidation. For me, one of the most disorienting aspects to being in the company of God has been coming to terms with my lack of advantage. I'm used to being in relationships in which I am able to leverage all manner of tangible and intangible things. That doesn't mean I'm a sinister character trying to take advantage of my people. When my son is running low on cash, I'm hardly taking advantage of him by handing him a twenty. I happily leverage my cash flow to help him out.

There are two streams of thought here that surface for me. One has to do with leveraging for the sake of position. This would mean that I use my advantage or influence to place myself in a position of power or control (maybe sinister, but most likely just practical and even appropriate).

The need I feel to be in a position of control or power is like a second skin to my natural self. It is a conversation we'll have a few chapters later, but for now, this concept provides context for the very real and common pursuit of relationships that include aspects where I have advantages the other person does not have. Our healthiest relationships include a balance of strengths and weaknesses, each person by virtue of his or her "advantages" complementing the other. We're attracted to others who possess characteristics or skills that we don't. The idea is that we are better for their strengths, as they are for ours.

My husband is an amazing, creative cook, so I'm spoiled to have my dinner made for me every evening. And I have a knack for technology, so I'm the IT person in the house. In the course of our relationship playing out, we leverage our strengths, enjoying the sense of control and the benefit of enhancing each other's life in the process. We need and appreciate the advantages each of us possesses.

It takes maturity to rightly appropriate advantages in the relationships we have because sometimes the power and control we possess *is* used in a sinister way, leveraged for the purpose of dominating or subduing another person. Children are inherently vulnerable—foster kids even more so. A high percentage of foster youth who age out of foster care (something that happens when they turn eighteen) become targets for evil men and women seeking to exploit them. They are targets precisely because they do not have the ability to leverage power on their own behalf.

For better or for worse, leverage, advantage, power, and control are part of every earthly relationship. We never move toward a person without consciously or subconsciously bringing our advantages with us. But when I occupy the fourth chair, I have no position to leverage anything at all. I'm not in a democratic setting in the company of God. There's no card in my pocket to play at an opportune moment so that I might gain the upper hand. There are no tactics I can employ to gain even the slightest advantage. Have you ever stayed away from the presence of God precisely because of the gross disadvantage you have? I have. Sometimes, Christians go into hiding so they do not have to face being powerless in God's presence.

My second thought regarding advantage in relationships has to do with the very understandable desire to contribute to meeting another person's needs. I like to be needed, and I like to meet needs. When I'm able, I like to leverage my resources for that purpose. But God is not in need in any measure. He has always been and remains complete within Himself. He has no need outside Himself. I've always understood that intellectually, yet still, I'll haul my bag of wares into God's company. I'm just egocentric enough to feel I might improve the quality of His existence. But without fail, each time I do that silly thing, I find Him complete already.

What do I make of the fact that God has no need of me, especially in light of my comprehensive need of Him? What do He and I do in this relationship in which He has no need of me? I'm so accustomed to thinking about the utilitarian aspects of my potential contribution to others. I have to intentionally remind myself that *this relationship is not like any other I've ever experienced.* I am one flawed and needy human paired with a perfect, thoroughly resourced, all powerful, sovereign, ubiquitous community of Three.

For quite a few years, this reality fell into the "spiritual tension" category for me. But as I became willing to practice holding that tension before God, He reshaped my thinking to reflect a truer picture of how He and I interrelate. He reminded me about another, far more compelling element of our connection. While God does not need me, desire overflows the banks of His heart and moves Him uninhibited in my direction. He loves me, and it is that love that drives Him toward me. My contribution to our relationship begins as my heart answers back in kind—desire meeting desire. Ultimately, it's far more compelling to be *desired* than *needed*. A choice born out of desire might be foreign to my human sensibilities, but as I grow in relationship with God, I find His pursuit of me all the more marvelous.

As I reflect back in time, my need to be needed was entirely bound up in a false sense of my own value. To feel good about being on the planet, *I needed to be needed.* Naturally, I applied that dynamic to the relationship God had invited me into. Slowly, that wrong thinking faded. The reality that God would invite me toward Him out of desire alone began to have the impact on my heart that it was always meant to have. Why does this matter? Because until that awareness settled soundly in me, grappling with God's lack of need for me kept me outside the inner circle of His fellowship.

I am altogether known by God. I am entirely exposed in His presence. I have literally nothing to leverage as I move toward Him. God knows me far better than I know myself. As disorienting as these realities have been, the most striking "disadvantage" I've wrestled with is this: God understands motive. God knows that very core thing within me that drives my choices, my reactions, and my behavior. That takes being known into a different stratosphere. If I could know something or someone entirely— that is to say, I could know every last detail about who they are—for all the advantage that would afford me, I still could not judge motive. Motive lies beneath the details, beneath behavior. Only God understands the *why* behind the details.

"For You, You only, know the hearts of all the children of mankind…"
—1 Kings 8:39

"But You, O LORD, know me; You see me, and test my heart toward You…"
—Jeremiah 12:3

[Your] *"eyes are open to all the ways of the sons of men…"*
—Jeremiah 32:19

"The LORD weighs the spirit."
—Proverbs 16:2

"The LORD searches all hearts and understands every intent of the thoughts."
—1 Chronicles 28:9, NASB

"For He knows the secrets of the heart."
—Psalm 44:21

"I am He who searches the minds and hearts."
—Revelation 2:23, NKJV

Over and over in the Bible, God proves He is primarily concerned with matters of the heart; with motives. In other words, He is concerned more with *why* you do the thing you do than He is with what you do. The heart exposes motive. That doesn't mean God turns a blind eye to my behavior; quite the contrary. But He's wise enough to understand that until I address the root cause of my behavior, I will likely keep repeating it.

Only God knows why I do what I do, think what I think, behave the way I behave. He knows why I'll resist something and why I'll run uninhibited toward another thing. He knows why I feel vulnerable with certain people and safe with others. He knows why I'm as bold as a lion in certain settings and running for shelter in others. And God understands all that's propping up the requests I make of Him. He knows what's hiding beneath the surface every single time I'm less than authentic, less than honest, or less than forthright. He knows when my heart is true, when my motives are pure, when I'm my most sincere self.

Phew! If these are new thoughts for you and they don't elicit some level of trepidation, check your pulse! That we would be frightened and reluctant as we consider the invitation to draw in and occupy the fourth chair is not just understandable; in my estimation, it's at least initially appropriate. I am a finite being considering approaching the infinite Triune God. The million-dollar question is this: Will I will recoil and hide, or will I press through the fear to see what this invitational God might reveal about His nature?

The children of Israel recoiled. In doing so, they made sure they would always have a person acting as a go-between. They forfeited the heart of the relationship God was offering them. In contrast, Moses pressed through His fear and experienced God in the most improbable way—Moses, the man, and God, the Maker of the man, meeting as friends.

God understands that if He has my heart, He has all of me. He's prepared to help me orient to a whole new way of thinking and being as I come into His presence. He's sympathetic to my lack of understanding about how to be with Him. He's ready to embrace me and teach me if I am willing to push past the fears inherent in "seeing" Him. There is no question He is offering Himself as my Chief Companion. There are so many beautiful aspects to that companionship. My needs are met. My desires are fulfilled. The soul space within me is satisfied with the One who was designed to occupy it. I was made to commune with the Living God. It's a fit that's hand-in-glove and perfectly synced.

The only friction possible in our relationship comes if I chafe against His leading, if I push back against Him. We also have an archenemy who understands this conversation all too well. He broke fellowship with God and never returned, unwilling to submit himself any longer to his Maker. Satan will enter the scene the moment he sees we are contemplating assigning the rights of our hearts to God, and he will do all within his power to knock us off that course. That can elicit a fear of its own that God may very well allow us to wrestle through until we mature in our ability to combat and defeat our adversary.

God has asked me to do some things as I've occupied the fourth chair that have caused me to shudder. "Let loose of that bitterness," He has said. "Stop punishing that person for sins long ago committed against you. Let Me pull that prop down. You've leaned on it far too long." I've heard His voice tell me, "Walk away from that idol. It's capturing your heart." Those rings of power I pretended weren't in my pocket, He thoughtfully, mercifully helped me pull out so that one by one, I could let them drop to the floor and finally be free of them.

I have also picked up new "rings" along the way, and God tends to them in His time and way because He does not want anything to break our fellowship. Sometimes, I simply don't want to cooperate. Sometimes, what's asked of me as I submit to His ways requires faith I do not yet possess. Sometimes, the war between my flesh and my spirit rages to the degree that I yield to my flesh and break fellowship with my Companion. That fracture lasts only as long as my willfulness persists. God stands ready to receive me again, His heart poised and eager to lavish His love on me (like the father of the prodigal son; see Luke 15:11–32).

Within the circle of four chairs, love and companionship of the richest kind is found. It has surpassed my best, most imaginative ideas of what communion with God might be like. It's not surprising, then, that the fight that I must engage in from time to time, is first to enter and then to protect that sacred, life-giving circle of four. In the inevitable moments of weakness that come as part of every life, I must be quick to instruct my own soul: remember the Company you keep, and *"Let us hold fast the confession of our hope without wavering, for He who promised is faithful"* (Hebr. 10:23).

Chapter 6

The Struggle to Enter
Why Wouldn't I Occupy My Chair?

"Draw near to God, and He will draw near to you..."
—James 4:8

James 4:8 is written in the context of a very strong caution to the early Church. It comes from James, the half-brother of Jesus. This letter to *"the twelve tribes in the Dispersion"* (James 1:1) was among the first of the New Testament to be written. The fledging Church was learning how to draw near to a God that, only decades earlier, was in their midst in human form. The radical work Christ accomplished made it possible to be in permanent, right standing with God for the first time since the fall of humankind. It also restored the possibility of entering into relationship with Him. We can't know the degree of the impact of such radical and comprehensive change for those first-generation Christians. They were learning to think and live differently than anyone before them had ever lived.

Also, Christ followers were learning to orient to the absence of an intermediary. They now had direct access to God. They were to consider themselves temples, both individually and collectively. God the Son walked with them, and now God the Spirit dwelled within them— literally. Jesus Himself told them that He and the Father would come and make their home in them (see John 14:23). To say they were having trouble navigating all these profound intangibles would be a gross understatement. They were the trailblazers for the rest of us, and they left us a legacy of both triumph and failure.

There was tremendous infighting among the brethren as they stumbled about in their disorientation. They were really struggling to separate themselves from a value system in opposition to the faith they embraced. The culture they were living in was hostile to their belief in Jesus. They were up against the dominate pagan religion of the day, as well as the Jews who did not believe Jesus was the Messiah. Thus, James wrote this very much-needed letter of caution and instruction. This was a serious dose of "truth in love." James was not pulling any punches for the severity of the need.

I'm reminded of a morning more than twenty years ago, when I saw my toddler leaning forward, prepared to insert a fork into the holes of an electrical outlet. My response was immediate and severe. We both cried afterward as I frightened him to tears with my yell to stop.

While we have had our Gospel for two-thousand-plus years, the climate we live in today is increasingly and uncomfortably reminiscent of that of the early Church. There is tremendous division within the Body of Christ. We are struggling to maintain the tenets of the faith. Some orthodox beliefs are going by the wayside for many Christians, as we profess to having become "enlightened." And our culture is hostile toward the Gospel of Jesus

Christ to an unprecedented degree. That means, very simply, our faith is being put to the test as never before.

Christians talk about it and discuss it in terms of the Church as a whole, but change happens one person at a time—one Christian at a time. Belief solidifies or collapses in the hearts of individuals. Until a thing I believe is truly put to the test, I cannot know for certain the quality of what I profess to be truth. Many souls are crushed to find their faith incinerated in the fiery furnaces of trials and tests.

Every era has its unique batch of homemade trials. At present, the Church is past the point of mental and emotional capacity. Social media is dripping with hate speech between Christ followers who stand in opposition to one another. People who sincerely love each other are at each other's throats. We are beyond spent. We are dangerously divided. We are operating as if we are powerless to combat the onslaught of invitations to hate rather than remain lovingly unified. We are, as the body of Christ, woefully off our game. We have wrapped our arms around the world's unrest, and we're a collective mess.

The influence of what the letter of James calls "the world" is extremely relevant as we talk about why we might struggle to occupy our place in God's presence. True fellowship with Father, Son, and Spirit flourishes in an environment of singularity of thought and heart. James is time and again calling out—it's impossible to be united with God while still holding onto the values of the world. They are entirely mutually exclusive to one another. James implores the Brethren to *"keep oneself unstained from the world"* (James 1:27). Why? Because *"friendship with the world means enmity with God"* (James 4:4).

What would keep people who understand the beauty of God's invitation to them from occupying their place in His presence? Why, knowing how highly personal that invitation is, would a person choose to stay away? I am increasingly convinced that whatever the specific reasons, they all find their root in this idea of integrating two ways of thinking, two value systems. James emphatically states that for our beliefs to be pure and undefiled before God the Father, we must keep ourselves unstained from the world.

Any belief I hold that finds itself outside the structure that God has laid out for living falls under the category of "the world." That system of thinking is ruled by our adversary and stands in direct opposition to the ways of God. The Bible clearly states that its end leads to death.

For many years, I've been asking the Lord a few hard questions: "How have the threads of the world's value system woven their way into my thinking so that they're intermixed with Your ways? How is that impacting the way I'm able to relate to You? Am I clipping my own wings without even knowing it?" Our personal behavior, in response to the unfolding of our lives, is usually loaded with clues.

I know a Christian who's tagged himself "a runner and a hider" who bolts from the presence of God under certain circumstances. When his heart becomes tender toward the Lord so that he moves in His direction, he is besieged with demonic attacks so formidable, they cripple him with fear. Once he reestablishes himself at a distance from God, the attacks cease. He lives his life on the periphery of God's presence, having Him in view but not enjoying the companionship possible. For him, this is *the* impassable impediment. He believes many right things about

God, but he also believes his adversary to be too great a threat to engage in battle, which he would have to do to defeat him. He lives crippled by the conflicting messages within his system of belief.

I can relate to another friend who says that when she was young in her faith, she was unable to move toward the presence of God because of her sense of personal unworthiness. While God was calling her to come to Him just as she was, she believed there was something within her character she must possess before she could be accepted by Him. Until she could tease out the faulty thinking, she would remain at a distance from God. She was understandably influenced by the world around her that taught her we *earn* our way into the graces of others. She naturally applied that thinking to the possibility of communing with God.

I know men and women whose lives are demanding, who refuse to move toward God because they fear He might further complicate an already blistering pace of life. Western culture has formed within many of us the idea that we ought to be squeezing as much as possible out of our time on the planet, and we do this on behalf of ourselves and our loved ones. That's a potent lure for the born overachiever, and it means doom for those with passive tendencies.

For those of us with a dozen plates spinning at all times, communing with God seems a luxury that goes into the retirement portfolio (Pandemics, recession, and the like are placing retirement in the luxury category for most people). Whose system of thinking is prevailing when we can't or won't slow down the bullet train of life in order to redirect it toward God? After all, He is the one who means to guide and counsel us through each moment of our lives.

The hard truth is, God will most likely "complicate" the construction of our personal empires. And once He's gotten our attention, He can begin to introduce us to a new way of thinking, thereby a new way of living. Do you think it's possible that God would take advantage of a global pandemic to redirect our attention? He's a beauty for ashes kind of God, after all.

There are people in my life so beaten down by the abuse of others, they cannot possibly imagine God would be any different. Even if He were kind initially, they believe He would ultimately come to substantiate that they were justifiably abused. The "scar tissue" on the psyche of abused people permanently reshapes them. Until God has a chance to demonstrate His altogether otherness and to show that He is not like any person they have known, they won't be able to help but apply to Him the sentiments of the strongest, most influential voices in their lives. There are throngs upon throngs of emotionally and physically damaged people, kept from the only One who can love them perfectly. Among our most courageous brothers and sisters are those who find their way into their fourth chair on the heels of the abuse of others.

Some people simply don't see what all the fuss is about and choose to remain lethargic about engaging with God. I cannot help but think about the old fable that tells the story of a frog blissfully swimming in a pot of tepid water that was slowly coming to a boil. He was cooked before he knew it, ignorant of the impending tragedy. He died listless and happy, but he wasn't supposed to have died at all!

Especially in our technologically driven age in which every hand holds a device, the population of people living in a lull has exploded across the globe. We now have masses upon masses of people hypnotized by having "entered" the screen before them. I just ordered new eyeglasses with a protective coating to guard against harmful blue-light exposure from technological screens.

There is an altering of what life once was and a hyper-growth of virtual life that we have never experienced in the history of the world. We, as a society, have not yet learned to harness this "portal." In the meantime, the blue-light-glaze on the eyes of humanity leaves us danger-ously outside the life-giving provision found only in the company of God.

Sometimes we stay away from God, not because of something that's happened to us or because of some false message we have integrated into what we believe. Sometimes, with our eyes open, we choose to exercise our God-given right to live under our own influence. We choose autonomy. We choose to self-govern primarily because we want that position of authority.

I have loads of my own experience of refusing to draw into God's presence simply because I did not want to be told what to do. I wanted the opportunity to exercise my will, use the mind I was given, come to my own conclu-sions about things, and make my own decisions. If you have parented a strong-willed child, you have no doubt been baffled by their short-sightedness. They are willing to invite all manner of trouble and hardship on themselves simply for the sake of exerting their right to be the one who chooses. I'd venture to say none of us has escaped that fleshly tendency; some of us would confess it remains a recurring theme throughout our lives.

Many of us are not so much self-governed as we are governed by various outside elements. The ruling force in our life might be anything from a particular drug of choice to alcohol or pornography. It might be a sports franchise, gambling or gaming, or any other thing that falls under the very broad category of addiction. Of course, the nature of addiction is that the substance/habit has become the controlling force in a person's life. It now drives behavior, decisions, and the use of resources. It has replaced healthy forms of life management and steers the affected person to "mask" rather than engage in their lives. These souls who find their way into the presence of God are also among our bravest. In His presence, they have put themselves in a position to be able to come out from under their addiction. God's arms are open wide, eager to receive those of us held captive in this way.

All of us, at different points in our journeys, have remained at a distance from God, preferring to cling to various sins. If I believe there is no hiding in His presence, and I don't want Him confronting the sin in my life, there's no way I want to slip into the fourth chair! The choice to cling to sin has so many dangerous layers. "How many days do I have on this Earth? What are the implications of remaining in my sin? Who might be dragged into the wake of my behavior and harmed?"

I have, in the past, deluded myself into thinking my poor choices were mine alone; therefore, no one else should be stained by them. The energy and time it took to first delude myself and then to maintain that delusion is time and energy I grieve to have squandered. I praise God that He loves to extend mercy. I praise Him for His eagerness to restore a repentant heart and for the truly staggering gift it is to be given a fresh start, even as one must navigate the fallout from having lived outside the will of God.

Some of us are so crippled by our past failures that shame keeps us from believing God would want us anywhere near Him. Adam and Eve were the first to experience shame in the aftermath of their disobedience in the Garden of Eden. The terrible soul dissonance they felt drove them instinctively into hiding. God pursued them, brought them out of hiding, and made provision for Adam and Eve to "cover their shame." He wants you and me to understand that shame should never keep us from His presence; rather, it should send us running to Him. He will lovingly address the source of our shame to lead us to repentance and restoration.

If our past sins have been dealt with before the Lord, we are forgiven, and God has wiped them away. He will never apply those failures to us again. *"Remember not the sins of my youth or my transgressions; according to Your steadfast love remember me, for the sake of Your goodness, O LORD!"* (Ps. 25:7). Our adversary knows how powerful and potentially debilitating it can be to "remind" us of past failures. He will do his best to entice us away from the presence of God by shaming us. Too many of us stay at a distance from God because we believe those damning, poisonous whispers. Shame is a powerful weapon of our enemy.

This is but a sampling of what I'm sure are innumerable reasons we might choose not to occupy our place in the presence of God. And most of our stories will include a vast array of reasons that ensure our fourth chair remains vacant. Does it matter? Does it really matter all that much that we would choose to live on the periphery of the presence of God? How dangerous can it be to maintain a short distance from the fourth chair? And before we move on from here, is there really a danger if we piecemeal together our system of beliefs, as long as God is well represented within that framework?

"Therefore, if anyone is in Christ, he is a new creation. The old has passed away; behold, the new has come" (2 Corin. 5:17). I too often succumbed to the familiar longings within my flesh, choosing not to move toward the circle of God's company. I often gravitated toward the familiarity of, and frankly the ease of flowing with, the ways of the world around me. All my natural sensibilities, combined with a culture that applauded and supported my autonomy, made is easy for me to "forget" I was a new creation, with a new standard to adhere to. That was keeping me out of His presence, out of the life-giving gift of His company. It also meant that I was dealing with constant emptiness and frustration.

The result of all this is that I was sincerely bewildered. "Why don't I sense Your presence, Lord? Where are You?" I began to cry out to Him to show me where He was. I would tell Him that He wasn't where I needed Him, that I needed to be able to find Him in my actual life. Was He hiding in the prayer closet when I really needed Him to help me parent or to be a better wife to my husband? Did He intentionally depart when I was in a conflict so that I shut down emotionally and looked like a fool? In time, and in His very kind way, He began to reveal that this "discrepancy" was not because He was unwilling to engage me but because I was straddling the fence between His Kingdom and the "kingdom" of man. I lived as if I had two primary residences.

Communing with God is not a lovely option that I can either exercise safely or not. I am in need. I am specifically, singularly in need of God. I am reliant on variables outside myself to sustain my life, variables God has put in place. I *"live and move and have my being"* (Acts 17:28) because God maintains the systems He created that make it possible for me to keep on living. I'm no less in need in my inner person.

If I'm made to commune with God, and have claimed Jesus as Lord of my life, then to live outside of His presence is to live cut off from the Source by which I am able to stay spiritually alive. I stay in spiritual infancy because I cannot mature apart from the Spirit of God in me. Nor can I make any kind of meaningful contribution to others without the counsel and provision of God. That is not the scenario God has in mind for my life.

When the apostle Paul told the Christians in Philippi, *"And my God will supply every need of yours according to His riches in glory in Christ Jesus,"* he was helping them understand this was possible only as they walked by the Spirit—as they occupied their place in His presence. I cannot simultaneously walk by the Spirit and walk by the flesh. They war against one another to the degree that you will want to do a right thing and not be able to do it if your flesh is in charge. The opposite, however, is a blessed truth— the flesh *cannot* prevail if I am walking by the Spirit.

James was the best kind of spiritual father to speak so plainly about the dangers inherent in blending value systems. He recognized that to be of two minds was to be unstable in all matters of life. And he was emphatic that there was no use in a double-minded person asking for wisdom from God because He would not be party to such duplicity. He would not be teaming up with other gods like He had a seat on the board of directors of a person's life. This isn't "mean God" refusing to play with others. This is Creator God, whose template for living has fixed parameters that must be adhered to if we are to experience abundant life now and forever.

Perhaps the most powerful ploy of our adversary is to lure those in the family of God away from His presence. He couldn't care less about why we would stay away, just that we do. As long as we are out from under God's influence, we are incapable of living as the new creations we are. We are out of position to be able to effect any change that might lead to true personal transformation. We cannot enter into the work of the Kingdom in our "flesh" because we need the Spirit of God in us to enable us. In a phrase, we remain entirely off the spiritual grid. It's a kind of self-imposed paralysis.

Why would we carry our God-given birthright in our back pockets and live as citizens of the world? Imagine the heartache of God, knowing the price He paid to purchase our freedom from the dominion of darkness, only to have His new creations going on as if nothing had changed. God's not trying to win a point (He will win every point, ultimately). His desire is to have those He deeply loves living under the sway of His Spirit, which is the way we were designed to live and mature.

James saw the danger growing in the early Church and urged them to make the shifts necessary to move toward God and settle there in His presence. There, they would be single-minded in their devotion to God, positioned to be comprehensively influenced by Him. This would be their path to fullness of life and joy. It is ours as well.

Where do you hesitate, so that you might choose *not* to draw near to God? Maybe there are more than a few areas you can identify. I urge you to begin a dialogue with God about them. I also urge you to speak to trusted friends who might see you more clearly than you are able to see yourself. Ultimately, any impediment keeping you from the life-giving presence of God is dangerous. God will be eager to help you navigate them for your good. The struggle to enter God's presence is real and common and one that every believer has to address through the course of his or her life.

When the Church is healthy, it provides an environment in which people can safely disclose their personal struggles and find the kind of support God intends for us to be for one another. We are meant to be in Christian community and suffer greatly if we are not. But even if you are not part of that kind of community, God still waits for you. He will have what you need in His hands to begin to deconstruct the false thinking you may have embraced. He will help you tease out the tangles so the blended systems of belief can be separated, and He will help you remove what is not reliable.

God, of His own will, *"brought us forth by the word of truth, that we should be a kind of firstfruits of His creatures"* (James 1:18). Truth brought us to life in Him. By His truth we will be freed from the bondage of falsehoods. Free people are healthy people, and they mature progressively and incrementally. They are more and more able to love God with their whole selves and to love others as Christ loves.

James's pleas were timely two thousand years ago and just as timely today. These words of caution were written not to unbelievers but to Christ followers. The urgency from James is unmistakable: *"What causes quarrels and what causes fights among you? Is it not this, that your passions are at war within you? You desire and do not have, so you murder. You covet and cannot obtain, so you fight and quarrel. You do not have, because you do not ask. You ask and do not receive, because you ask wrongly, to spend it on your passions. You adulterous people! Do you not know that friendship with the world is enmity with God? Therefore whoever wishes to be a friend of the world makes himself an enemy of God"* (James 4:1–4). Such strong language! But how ultimately kind to sound the alarm in such a way that would elicit the abrupt change of course so desperately needed.

James did not leave "the twelve tribes in the Dispersion" alarmed but without direction. What was his remedy? How did he instruct them so they might turn from their present course? He implored them to humble themselves before God, to submit themselves to God, to draw near to God. He was instructing them to move in God's direction and take their place within His presence.

He, led by the Spirit of God, pleaded with them to see the error and danger of friendship with the world. It was keeping them out of the circle of His company. He asked them to move humbly toward the One they must be influenced by to become the men and women they were made to be. The remedy set down for them is our remedy as well.

May God help each of us to see where we are in need. He asks only that we open ourselves to Him. The work of transformation is His. The ability to be freed from binding untruths is a work done by His Spirit. But that work cannot even begin until we slip into our chair, in the company of Father, Son and Spirit. May we cooperate with Him by laying at His feet any and all impediments that have kept us from Him, open to including those we are yet unaware of. May we grow in our appetite for Him and no other, eager to live out our days under His pervasive and perfect influence.

"Oh, how abundant is Your goodness,
which You have stored up for those who fear You
and worked for those who take refuge in You,
in the sight of the children of mankind!
In the cover of Your presence You hide them
from the plots of men;
You store them in Your shelter
from the strife of tongues.
Blessed be the LORD,
for He has wondrously shown His steadfast love
to me when I was in a besieged city."
—Psalm 31:19–21

Chapter 7

The Struggle for Power
Loss of Control

*"If anyone would come after Me, let him deny
himself and take up his cross daily and follow Me."*
—Luke 9:23

*"That we gain heaven,
that we are delivered from sin,
that we are made useful to God -
these things never enter as considerations
into real abandonment, which is a
personal sovereign preference
for Jesus Christ Himself."*
—Oswald Chambers

What if life in the fourth chair was nothing more than a safe, snuggly place to be cared for and doted on by God? What if its primary purpose was for the advancement of my happiness? My very selfish soul wouldn't so much mind the idea of occupying it. Even if some degree of service were required, or if there were some kind of dues to pay; if it was for *my* good and happiness,

I'd comply without too much grumbling. Even if I had to adopt a vocabulary careful to elevate God—if, in reality, *my* personal comfort and advancement were actually the objective—I'd cooperatively use my best God language and comply.

But what if, instead, I found that occupation of the fourth chair required my complete surrender, so that my flesh would no longer rule—my reason no longer be able to come to bear? Moreover, my desire for happiness would be laid aside entirely for some higher purpose, and I would learn to be concerned not at all with myself but with God and what was important to Him. Truth be told, at that point, the chair would seem much more like an electric chair, complete with leather cuffs for ankles, waist, and wrists, and a blindfold. I'd most likely be screaming, *"Not happening!"*

For a fairly long period of my life, mostly subconsciously, and without the language I used above, I fought the occupation of the fourth chair. Instead, I invented and maintained an alternate reality that included God, mostly where I felt it was doable to include Him, leaving sections of my life under my control. I would promise God, of course, that I would use my best managerial skills to take very good care of those omitted sections (I felt I should assure Him). I was really completely in control, with God heading up the areas I said He could be in charge of. If I'm honest, that's what I saw most other Christians doing. It was, therefore, extremely easy to create my spiritual virtual reality.

The image in my mind is of two superhighways, both heading north, aligned so they are side by side with only a hair's breadth between them. All the lanes are heading the same direction. I'm in charge, and sometimes I allow the two to slightly overlap, allowing the God superhighway to converge with the Anne superhighway. These slight intersections would mark my most spiritual moments in life. But then the superhighways would move back to their hair's-breadth distance, and I would resume my normal life.

Because the God superhighway was so near, so clearly in view, I contented myself with the thought that I was indeed one of God's best followers—that this was what life as a Christian should look like. I was amply supported by other God integrators. There were occasional fringe, extreme Christians with only one superhighway, and they were missionaries or radicals of another ilk (whom I deeply admired). I felt a little sad not to be one of them. But I wasn't. I wasn't one of them. I was a regular Christian.

These past ten years, as I've descended deeper into the depths of the metaphor of the four chairs, and as I've meditated on the Word of God, I've come to an abrupt impasse with that familiar "integrated" spiritual existence. Rather than finding support for it, I'm seeing over and over, with vivid clarity, there is in fact no meaningful reality other than total surrender to God—the total, complete abdication of control of one's life to God. For a Christian, any other reality is a false one.

If you would have asked me if God was in control of my life or did I feel as though He should be, my answer would have been unhesitatingly yes. On the surface I believed I was actually living that life. It's just that I'd keep hitting rough patches where God didn't seem to be cooperating with me. I didn't have the maturity to see that He had a different agenda than I did. I wouldn't even have been able to ascertain there were two agendas in play.

I was like one of those crazy traders on the floor of the New York Stock Exchange, waving paper in the air and yelling out orders to buy and sell, all with the intent of smartly managing my portfolio. I'd diversify precisely for the purpose of not going bankrupt should one of my investments turn belly-up. In human terms, there's something very sensible about this approach. I've practiced it. I'm sure I still am in pockets of my life.

But I kept trying to picture myself slipping into my fourth chair, knowing I'd hedged my assets, knowing I wasn't all-in. And I kept trying to look into the face of God to see if He knew I wasn't all-in, to see if He was going to let me play this game with Him. And my gut felt terrible because how on Earth *could* He be OK with me playing that game? I was truly awakening to the fact that I was essentially using Him to advance my quality of life, biding my time until I could go to heaven.

I have loved God since I was a little girl. I have asked Him to make me a woman of character, to have His way in my life, whatever that might mean. And He, in response, has been slowly revealing Himself to me. He has also been slowly, kindly, revealing *me* to me. I remember in my early thirties attending a three-day retreat at a monastery a few hours from my home. One afternoon, I had several uninterrupted hours in a little chapel. I was alone there with God. It was peaceful and quiet, which was such a rarity. My pragmatic brain was eager to meet with God, and I literally prepared a list (I had the piece of paper in my hand) of things that God might possibly want to address with me.

Each thing on the list was a fair assessment (according to me) of different circumstances in my life that were difficult and that I hoped God would rectify. There were people I hoped He would reprove (according to me) so that my life would improve. There were injustices (according to me) that I felt sure He would want to address and make right. There was imbalance in the way my life was constructed (according to me) that I knew He would want to bring into balance, if only He and I had a little time to "talk things through and make a new plan." I'm positive I had them written in order of priority, but I was open to God rearranging them if He wanted to. So, list in hand, I waited. I listened. And God spoke to my spirit.

Shockingly (I was truly bewildered), not only did He not address anything on my list, He turned His attention to the last thing I thought He could possibly be concerned about. He addressed the condition of my heart. One definitive sentence dropped in my consciousness, as if God sat beside me using His best English: "Anne, you have no idea the depth of the deceitfulness of your own heart." I sat quietly, waiting for Him to retract it, redirect, and choose something to discuss from my list. But I heard nothing beyond that sentence. I lingered in that little chapel for some time, waiting and wondering what on Earth I was to do with what I had "heard."

That ended up being among the most significant moments of my spiritual journey. For about thirty-years now, God has been fleshing-out for me what He meant and why that statement was the *only* thing I needed to hear that day. I should also say that while that was a very disorienting and confusing thing to be confronted with, I felt His love and kindness. He was not even rebuking me. He was, however, beginning to open my mind to how upside-down my thinking was as it pertained to Him and what it meant to be in relationship with Him.

"Have Your way in me, whatever it means!" That's a

prayer perfectly aligned with His will. And I had exactly zero idea of what it would mean to have that prayer answered. I had zero idea of how much of my belief system was a blending of the demands of my flesh and the desire of my spirit. I really didn't understand at all. But I needed to understand. God knew it and had every intention of bringing me to a precipice where I could view this absurd dual superhighway.

He knew I was largely unaware of what I was doing. He knew I had no idea the danger of succumbing to the insatiable thirst within my flesh to be in control at all costs or the fact that I was essentially grafting Him into my plan for my life. At the same time, He knew my spirit was willing but that my "flesh" was still prevailing. He knew that for many years to come, I would keep constructing the framework of my existence according to the appetites of my flesh. But He also knew that ultimately, He would prevail as I progressively understood what it meant to dethrone myself and relinquish the crown and scepter to Him.

I was ignorant. But I was "in," no matter what. I felt as if I could hear Him in response to my cry. "Have your way God, whatever it means!"

And God would reply, "Great. It's just that for that to happen, I have to be completely in charge. You have to allow Me access to every part of who you are. You have no idea how many layers deep the plans are that you've made for yourself. I'll show them to you, and you'll have to release your grip on them entirely. I'll have to help you do that. I have to help all my children do that. It's not in your flesh to yield to Me. But you won't start truly living until you do. So My Spirit in you will empower you to place the whole of who you are into My hands. I will take far better care of you than you are able to take care of yourself."

It was often excruciating to come to terms with another layer of my me-centered universe. I began to wonder if I had ever, even once, had a thought that was not ultimately about my own personal advancement.

In retrospect, I can imagine no other path but the one I've traveled and continue to travel. What did I think it meant to be transformed into the likeness of Christ? That's the path every Child of God is on. I know now that, in part, it means I'm gradually dying to the pursuit of my own well-being and comfort. It also means I'm progressively coming alive, walking as the new creation I am.

The struggle for power; for control of the reigns of one's life, is the battle of all battles in the life of a follower of Christ. It lies at the core of every war waged between the flesh and the spirit. Nothing flies in the face of human reason more than that a person would, of his or her own free will abdicate total control of his or her life to God. Yet God requires it from the person who would follow Him. He requires it of me. Occupancy of the fourth chair comes with a caveat issued consistently throughout Jesus's public life. The Gospels of Matthew, Mark, and Luke all contain the statement Jesus made that if I would follow Him, I *must* deny myself and daily take up my cross—two impossible acts of selflessness apart from the intervention of God the Spirit in me.

I sometimes forget that Jesus, by emptying Himself and *"taking the form of a servant"* (Phil. 2:7), placed Himself in the same impossible position I find myself. He was showing me what it looks like and what's possible when the will bows and the control of one's life is placed in the hands of God. Jesus did nothing of Himself. He was never operating under any agenda except that of God the Father. He relied on the Father's power to carry out the Father's will. In His own words He confessed, "I can of myself do nothing." Eventually, Jesus took up His literal cross and, by the power of the Spirit of God, fulfilled the purpose for which He became human.

Who will be in control of my life? God will be as I submit the whole of who I am to Him, relinquishing control of my life. I submit the will He gave me to His will so that He is in fact the controlling force in my life. He makes the decisions. He guides me to people and places, and He is in charge so that my responses to those people and situations are shaped and formed by God the Spirit, who lives in me.

With His help, I wrestle through the impediments that keep me at a distance from Him. I trust Him to open up, dismantle, or deconstruct any false thinking I've allowed to inform my decisions to stay away from Him. And I'm clear about the fact that to occupy my place in His presence is to purpose to submit the entirely of myself to His comprehensive influence. I do that because I trust that God is entirely good, having only my best in mind and being the *only* One to bring that best to fruition. This is what it mean to walk by the Spirit. This is the singular posture that allows me to live as the new creation I am.

Jesus's life teaches me something else that turns this whole conversation about control on its head. It would be enough that He practiced living fully submitted to the Father, but driving that submission was not the advancement of self, or the even the fulfillment of His purpose for coming to the Earth. The driving force—the thing that motivated His behavior—was His abiding love for the Father. It's here where Oswald Chamber's statement quoted at the beginning of the chapter hits me like a punch in the gut. Just about the time I'm settling in to the need for the release of control, I'm faced with a deeper consideration still: "What is driving me to release control? What's motivating my behavior?" As Chambers so eloquently stated, there is no consideration that ought to drive me into the company of God but "a personal sovereign preference for Jesus Christ Himself."

I'm coming closer to that most elusive and primary discovery. Whom do I love? Who has my heart? If I had the power to move heaven and Earth, whom would I elevate so that the whole world could see the One I love? God is relational at His very core, in loving community with the three Persons who make up His essence. The Triune God is reaching for me for relationship that would ultimately emulate what exists within Himself. He's inviting me to love Him as He loves me. He's commanded me, as His child, to love Him with the whole of my being; with all my heart and soul and mind and strength.

My acts of submission are ultimately meant to be fueled by my love for Him and my desire to please Him. But I do not possess within myself an ability to be selfless, to love someone more than I love myself. If I'm going to truly love God, I'm going to need His love to do it. And I can, as I subjugate my heart to His and let His love come alive in me. *"Love is from God, and whoever loves has been born of God and knows God"* (1 John 4:7). Even the love He requires for Himself must come from Him.

In the struggle for power, only one of us is struggling. God is not struggling. God is patiently reaching for me. He is eager to demonstrate His love for me. If love is not what is motivating me to take my place in the fourth chair, I will find myself loath to remain in His company. I will find myself slipping out of my chair, breaking fellowship with Him. I have found God to be full of mercy as I have treated my fourth chair like a hot seat, darting in and out according to the prevailing object(s) of my passion. I shouldn't wonder that I am dependent on Him to cultivate the field of my heart, that it might produce a harvest of gratitude, love, and passion for Him.

Now that the Spirit of God has hold of me, and as I experience the quality of His love through my submission to Him, I find my heart reshaped. I make more of my decisions to safeguard the union between Him and me. I find I'm fighting to preserve that unity. I find my heart more and more longing to please Him, honor Him, and love Him as He loves me.

> *"As a deer pants for flowing streams, so pants my soul for You, O God. My soul thirsts for God, for the living God…By day the LORD commands His steadfast love, and at night His song is with me, a prayer to the God of my life."*
> —Psalm 42:1–2,8

Chapter 8

The Struggle to Stay
Why Would I Leave?

"For I do not understand my own actions. For I do not do what I want, but I do the very thing I hate."
—Romans 7:15

"For we do not wrestle against flesh and blood, but against the rulers, against the authorities, against the cosmic powers over this present darkness, against the spiritual forces of evil in the heavenly places."
—Ephesians 6:12

W hy would any rational child of God ever leave the safety and sanctuary of fellowship with God? Why, having relinquished control to God would I ever seek to put myself back under the sway of my narrow thinking? Why would I invite danger by coming out from the stronghold God provides for me, making myself an open target for my adversary? To slip out of the fourth chair is nothing shy of self-sabotage. No sane person would do this to themselves. Yet I find myself periodically slipping out of my chair, and operating not as one who has *"died to sin"* (Romans 6:2), but rather as my *"old self"* (Rom. 6:6).

"For the death He died He died to sin, once for all, but the life He lives He lives to God. So you must also consider yourselves dead to sin and alive to God in Christ Jesus" (Rom. 6:10-11). The Apostle Paul goes on to say in Romans 8:2, *"For the law of the Spirit of life has set you free in Christ Jesus from the law of sin and death."* He tells me I'm to consider myself dead to sin and alive to God; that I'm set free from the laws of sin and death. It's unsettling at the very least to acknowledge that I have the ability to live as if I'm not free so that, *"I do not do what I want, but I do the very thing I hate"* (Rom. 7:15). In this Paul is describing the plight of every child of God this side of heaven.

When I think of spending the bulk of my years coming to terms with who ought to be in control of my life, I breathe a heavy sigh both of deep gratitude for God's patience, and sorrow for the years that feel to me as though they were squandered. Squandered because frankly, I had hoped to be less selfish than I actually am. Squandered because I had hoped I was more reasonable, more pliable in God's hands than I have been. Squandered because I had hoped I was someone who actually loved God as much as I said I did.

I don't imagine God thinks about me as having squandered decades while I slowly awakened to the depth of my preoccupation with self, or wrestled through my iron-clad determination to be in control. I have an idea that God was simply doing for me what He does for all His children. The end game is the same for all of us, that we would settle in to the fourth chair, in fellowship with

God, and truly live. But the path to that end is unique to each person.

What isn't unique is the war every child of God wages to remain in fellowship; to remain in the fourth chair. Finding my way into the fourth chair is not a once-and-for-all-time endeavor. In other words, I can break fellowship with God. I am not implying a break in the relationship I have with Him. I am eternally bound to God through faith in Jesus, and I am secure as His child. But I can and do find that I can put myself at odds with Him so that I am not enjoying the fellowship offered when He is in control of my life.

What does this fellowship look like? I can be in the company of someone and not be in fellowship with them. I have meandered in my son's bedroom while he's gaming, asked him questions that he actually answered, and then left his room without him ever being conscious that I was there. So it's not so much about proximity as it is about having someone's attention and them having yours. To be in fellowship is to be intentionally occupied with the one you're with. But fellowship with God has a significant component not present in my earthly relationships. Not only must God have my full attention, He must also occupy the position of power in the relationship. He's my King, after all.

The famous account of Simon Peter walking toward Jesus on the water might seem like an odd story to make this point. But for me, it paints the picture in pretty dramatic fashion. In Matthew 14, we read that Peter is literally walking on water during a sea-storm. That was happening as Peter was intently focused upon Jesus. The Son of God was in control and because of that Peter was experiencing something that wasn't supposed to be possible.

Before long, Peter is understandably distracted by the storm. The passage says, *"when he saw the wind, he was afraid, and beginning to sink he cried out!'"* (Matthew 14:30). For Peter to see the wind, he had to look away from Jesus. One fearful glance at it and fellowship broke. Once Peter focused on the source of his fear he immediately began to sink, and the natural world and its laws took over. That's quite a swing of the pendulum. Thankfully what Peter did next teaches me how to remedy a situation like that. Peter quickly cried out, *"Lord save me!"* Immediately Jesus reached out and drew him out from under the water. The connection and the supernatural power of God flowing into Peter was restored.

When Jesus had Peter's full attention as well as His full cooperation, he was safe, even though the storm raged around them. That's a powerful note-to-self. If I pause and think, I can nearly always count multiple storms around me either brewing or in full form. Allowing myself to become occupied by them rather than Jesus is all it takes for me to slip out of the safety and protection found in the fourth chair.

Why does God need to be in charge during the storms? The Apostle Paul said in Romans chapter seven that with his flesh he served the law of sin because that is essentially all the flesh is capable of. It shouldn't surprise me to have my natural-self— my flesh, do what flesh does when it's not under the sway of the Holy Spirit. Paul clearly states, *"For those who live according to the flesh set their minds on the things of the flesh, but those who live according to the Spirit set their minds on the things of the Spirit"* (Rom. 8:5).

When Peter was walking on the water he did not yet possess God the Spirit as he would beginning at Pentecost. But that night Peter *was* in the presence of God the

Son. As he stayed focused on Jesus, he was living *"according to the Spirit,"* under God's sway, which in that instance made him impervious to the laws of nature. When Peter *"saw the wind,"* he, in an instant, *"set his mind on the things of the flesh."*

As I was becoming more conscious of the power my flesh could wield even as a new creation in Christ, I started asking the Lord this question, *What's causing me to "see the wind" so that I'm breaking fellowship with You?*

I wrote a blog series several years ago that I ended up tagging *Suitors*. Any person or thought or outside-influence that would vie for my heart's attention I began to consider a Suitor. I started thinking about what a suitor does, how they do it, and what it is they are ultimately wanting from me. I started running that grid through every detail of each day, from the moment I opened my eyes in the morning to my last conscious thought before I fell asleep that night. I practiced that process for months, asking God to teach me. I thought about what I was dreaming during the night too— what was waiting in my subconsciousness that would only surface when I was asleep.

Practically, that meant I started paying attention to what I was paying attention to— to what had the power to distract me or lure me away from the fourth chair. I had to start asking myself, *What are some of the obvious dangers around me where my need of God is vividly apparent? Am I crying out to Him in those moments?* I also had to ask, *What are the less obvious dangers around me where I'm in trouble before I'm even aware of the danger?*

One very practical shift I made as the Lord showed me where I was easily distracted was in the area of entertainment. I began to think about what I was reading, watching, and listening to. What was the quality of the content I was taking in and did it serve to protect my environment so that I was comfortable remaining in the fourth chair, in fellowship with God? Entertainment was a category of life that I was completely in charge of, and I was functioning out of habit and little conscious thought. When I started thinking about it and inviting God into the choices I was making, I found adjustments that needed to be made. I made those adjustments, determined not to keep sabotaging fellowship with the Lord. I have never for a moment been sorry for removing any media content that had the ability to either clutter my thoughts or worse case, disturb a peaceable connection with God.

Am I comfortable engaging in x-y-z in the company of God? Is what I'm about to say or do something that I can engage in without impairing the harmony I experience in God's presence? These aren't questions I launch into thin air. When I ask them, I'm actually asking the Holy Spirit if I'm about to place myself in harm's way. If the answer is yes, I have a simple (but perhaps not easy) choice to make. Those choices will reveal whether my flesh is prevailing or whether I am open to being influenced by the Spirit of God. One response preserves fellowship with Him, the other finds me having vacated the fourth chair.

I began to view the desires of my flesh as perhaps my most formidable suitor. Not that I would become a woman without desire, but that God would be invited in to those desires and have the freedom to shape them so that they would reflect my new nature as a child of God. I resisted that for many years, not wanting God, as my friend likes to say, "all up in my business." But He *had* to be that driving force in shaping me or I would have continued to live as a spiritual infant, succumbing to the constant battle my flesh wages with my spirit. It is a war I will fight for the rest of my days, but as my trust in God grows, so does my resistance to my old nature.

Peter's instinct to be safe over-rode his ability to remain engaged with Jesus on the stormy sea, and Jesus challenged him about it. I have multiple-thousands of those kinds of moments in my own story. If Peter could have cried out to Jesus before he looked away, Jesus would have been able to encourage him to trust Him with his safety. I find it interesting that God rescued Peter and put him back in the boat before He calmed the storm. He did not eliminate the danger. He showed Peter His power in the face of it.

The relationship between Jesus and Peter gives us a look at the other broad stream of thought regarding why we might slip out of the fourth chair. This time it is not so much about Peter's battle with his flesh, rather it's about the war we wage with what the Apostle Paul calls principalities and powers. Paul says, in Ephesians six that we *wrestle* with all manner of unseen forces. These forces, like my old nature, come seeking to redirect my attention and ultimately my allegiance. If I succumb to them, they will capture my focus and bring doubt and mis-trust in God. If that happens, I will gravitate back to the ways of my old nature which is precisely their objective.

Right on the heels of the last meal Jesus shared with His closest companions before His death, Scripture records an exchange between Jesus and Peter. Peter's name was once Simon Bar-Jonah. Jesus gave him the name Peter after his confession that he believed Jesus to be *"the Christ, the Son of the living God"* (Matt. 16:16). Here's the conversation: *"Simon, Simon, behold, Satan demanded to have you, that he might sift you like wheat, but I have prayed for you that your faith may not fail. And when you have turned again, strengthen your brothers." Peter said to Him, 'Lord, I am ready to go with You both to prison and to death.' Jesus said, 'I tell you, Peter, the rooster will not crow this day, until you deny three times that you know Me'"* (Luke 22:31–34).

Jesus is telling Peter what's going to happen within the next handful of hours. Peter is vehemently disputing that prophetic word. That gives us insight into the level of Peter's general lack of awareness of principalities and powers. Peter seems to have glossed over the revelation that Satan had asked for him specifically. All Peter's mind could grasp was that Jesus said he would deny Him. He was in sweet fellowship with Jesus. It was inconceivable to Peter that he could do anything to jeopardize that connection.

What Peter would learn through that very painful experience of abandoning Jesus is that his will alone was not enough to keep him from causing disharmony in their relationship. Furthermore, he was in no way prepared to battle an unseen enemy. This is a reality I must also come to terms with because while I acknowledge my flesh as being the contentious thing that it is, my adversary is ever seeking my spiritual demise. I must practice submitting my will to the will of God. I must practice resisting the invitations from outside suitors meaning to capture my attention. And I must be watchful, aware that Satan seeks those he might devour.

Both stories about Peter ultimately became opportunities for him to learn about the quality of His faith in Jesus. In both instances Peter was still very young in that regard. Jesus tells him after He pulls him out the stormy sea, that he has *"little faith."* In this scene in the Upper

Room, Jesus lets Peter know He's going to be praying that his *"faith will not fail."* Peter's faith *did* fail later that night and he would suffer bitterly for it. Satan had his way in that instance, but God would teach Peter how to combat his adversary so that, *"the gates of hell could not prevail"* (Matt. 16:18) against him.

What does faith in God have to do with remaining in the fourth chair? If my faith is the measure of my trust in God and in the things God says are true, I should find myself practicing an ever increasing awareness of not only the war my flesh will wage with my spirit, but also of the reality of those things that are "unseen."

Both my flesh and my adversary are bent on keeping the fourth chair empty. I must, as Peter would caution later in his life, be *"sober-minded; be watchful. Your adversary the devil prowls around like a roaring lion, seeking someone to devour. Resist him, firm in your faith"* (1 Peter 5:8–9). Peter's denial of Jesus bore witness to this admonition, and he would do all in his power to encourage the fledgling Church not to fall in that same kind of trap.

We are thoroughly resourced by God to combat both our flesh and our adversary so that we can remain in the fellowship of His company. God is generous not only to caution us through his Word, but to equip us as well. If I walk by the spirit, it is literally impossible to *"gratify the desires of the flesh"* (Gal. 5:16). As I *"put on the full armor of God"* (Eph. 6:11), I am able to not only recognize but also *"stand against the schemes of the devil."*

To imagine myself sitting in the fourth chair, in that place of full submission, is a picture of walking in the Spirit and of fulfilling the apostle Paul's mandate to *"In all circumstances take up the shield of faith, with which you can extinguish all the flaming darts of the evil one; and take the helmet of salvation, and the sword of the Spirit, which is the word of God, praying at all times in the Spirit, with all prayer and supplication"* (Eph. 6:16–18).

May God renew a desire and commitment within us to avail ourselves of the lavish provision we find in the Word of God, so that we not only take our place in His company, but fight the inevitable battles to remain in the fourth chair. When we do, we will begin to settle hand-in-glove, into the space we were designed to occupy, in the fellowship of the One for whom we were made. We will have come home, in the deepest and truest sense.

> *"O may these heavenly pages be*
> *My ever dear delight;*
> *And still new beauties may I see,*
> *And still increasing light.*
> *Divine Instructor, gracious Lord,*
> *Be Thou forever near;*
> *Teach me to love Thy sacred Word,*
> *And view my Savior there."*

—"Father of Mercies," a hymn written by Anne Steele in 1760

Part 3

Coming Home
The Familial Connection

*"How lovely is Your dwelling place, O Lord of
hosts! My soul longs, yes, faints for the courts of
the LORD; my heart and flesh sing for joy to the
living God."*
—Psalm 84:1–2

The longing for home lives at the core of every human.
The sons of Korah, credited with penning this psalm,
understood where home was and why one's soul would
faint for longing to be there.

The invitation to occupy the fourth chair is nothing
less than a call to come home. The implications are staggering. So radical is the experience of being home that
many of us pass on the invitation simply because we have
no substantive frame of reference that makes it seem
possible. We walk away because it seems inconceivable
that God would have a spot in His company specifically
for us, where we would experience the fullness of what it
means to be alive, in relationship with Him.

If we polled a thousand people asking them to define

"home," we might find a wide spectrum of preferences. Yet nearly all would agree that *true* home includes another someone with whom we enjoy harmonious relationship and a richer experience of life. Synonymous with that, this other someone knows us altogether and loves us as we are.

That home is found in the company of God. It is there and only there that we find our deepest relational needs abundantly met. Only there, in fellowship with God, have we settled into the Company we were created to be in. The sensibility of this union with Him is well supported on two fronts. We come as image bearers, to the One whose image we bear. And we come as family members, sharing a spiritual DNA with God, having been grafted in to His family through faith in Christ Jesus.

We also come as people indwelled by the Holy Spirit, our bodies being temples that He resides in. There is no possibility of a more intimate and literal connection with another Being than the one a Christian shares with God. There is, therefore, no greater experience of fulfillment to be found than when a Christian takes his or her place in the fourth chair and settles into the sweetness of relationship found with Father, Son, and Spirit.

The wrestling we must do to rid ourselves of whatever keeps us from that fellowship is a nonnegotiable pursuit. We do it in reverence for God before we do it for ourselves. That it benefits us is secondary. It is an act of worship and an acknowledgment of His Divinity. We move toward "I am" in response to His invitation to come. The benevolent King has extended His scepter, and it is safe to draw near. When we do, we come home.

"Even the sparrow finds a home, and the swallow a nest for herself, where she may lay her young, at your altars, O Lord of hosts, my King and my God. Blessed are those who dwell in Your house, ever singing Your praise! Selah…For a day in Your courts is better than a thousand elsewhere."
—Psalm 84:3–4,10

Chapter 9

My Greatest Dream
Fully Known, Fully Accepted

> *"And I will ask the Father, and He will give you another Helper, to be with you forever. You know Him, for He dwells with you and will be in you...If anyone loves Me, he will keep My word, and My Father will love him, and We will come to him and make Our home with him."*
> —John 14:16–17,23

I've listened to more than a few Christian philosophers and theologians talk about the idea of what it means to be truly human. They roughly frame it like this: that to live as a true human, people must be engaged in the things that a human was created for. That includes fulfilling the purpose for which they were created. It also means they are in fellowship with God, who created them. The flip side is this—that a person lives in the shadows of his or her humanity until those criteria are in place and active. Any alternate version of life will be incomplete.

The image put forward in the early chapters of Genesis paints the picture of a man and woman created by God to steward those things God put under their jurisdiction and to fellowship with Him and one another in the context of creation. As that took place, Adam and Eve were living fully human, experiencing everything God intended for them to experience. They were living in the fullness of what it meant to be human. God was glorified by them and through them. Until sin entered the world, there was never a question as to whether humans would live as God intended.

As I occupy my place in the fourth chair, I enter the single place where I can be truly and fully human. There in the company of God, I live in the fullness of who I was made to be. Perhaps the most compelling word that sums up this right occupation is the word "home." I am living as a true human when I am home, in the company of God. In John chapter 14, Jesus comforts His followers by assuring them that not only will the Spirit live in them after He leaves, but that He and the Father would make their home in them.

The Greek word for "home" is monē, and it translates like this: *a staying, abiding, dwelling, or abode.* Modern dictionaries use this language: *shelter, center of domestic affections, dwelling place, retreat, refuge, native residence.* This gives us some insight into the uniqueness of home, so there are not multiple places that would suffice. There would be a singular place, and whether or not I occupied it, it would be *my* home. Jesus used the same word to describe both the home His Father was preparing in Heaven and the home He and the Father would have *in* His followers. I find that fact wondrous and very comforting.

If we could "peer" through the window of our true home, we would see a community/family in which we are deeply loved and championed. We would see ourselves not only receiving vital contributions but making our own vital contributions to those within the walls of our home. The substance of home is first relational. Part of being home is the very real experience of being in relationship with God, who knows me altogether and loves me as I am. While He desires my growth and directs me toward maturity, He does not do that so He can love me more. His comprehensive love for me is the driving force behind His encouragement of my growth and sanctification. We parent our children *because* we love them, not so that we *might* love them. That gives us a faint understanding of the quality of the love of God for His children and also an idea of why He spurs us on to become the mature children He's made us to be.

What are those of us up to who have not yet settled into the company of God? At the core of each of us is the innate desire to be fully known, fully accepted, and fully loved as we are. Akin to that is the need to contribute to something outside ourselves. We spend the best of ourselves searching for that. To the degree that hope lives, we keep searching. As hope wanes, we mask ourselves in some ways to dull the pain of not having found our way home yet. As we risk and/or mask, we inevitably collect wounds that impact us deeply. Once that happens, most of us begin to alter our innate perceptions of what home should be like, and we start searching for a livable alternative.

Our deepest inner wounds will always be relational wounds—those we have acquired through our experiences with other people. Those wounds tend to inform or reform our perceptions about what home might really look like. On any given day in the county where I live, there are approximately eight hundred kids in the foster-care system. These kids have lived through every imaginable and unimaginable horror of family or the lack of family. It's not uncommon to find girls as young as thirteen or fourteen willingly allowing themselves to become pregnant, desperate to create a family of their own. With an underdeveloped mind, and a trail of trauma behind them, little girls reach for the prospect of home with zero understanding of the implications of their actions.

Similarly, foster teens are incredibly easy prey for sex traffickers, in part because there is no frame of reference for what a healthy *home* looks like. Sinister adults lure them in much the same manner as those who lure children into gang life. They offer the promise of *family*. Desperately lonely, vulnerable children are no match for the open arms of another human being, even one intent on exploiting them.

But relatively healthy men and women also search for home in ways that cannot possibly meet the core needs within them. To varying degrees, each of us settles for a lesser experience of home rather than pressing on toward the One who calls us into harmonious union with Himself.

If I look very honestly at my own heart, I find it still hesitates at times, believing it will be letting go of a tangible expression of true home if I slip into the fourth chair. I recognize the ambiguity of that statement, but what I'm getting at is this: I want the fullness of the experience of home, meaning I want to be truly loved and fully accepted as I am, *and* championed, *and* empowered to thrive...by/with another human. I can't see God. I *can* see another human. I can't touch God. I *can* touch another human. My chair is, after all, as metaphoric as the three that God occupies. I long for tangible, visceral human interaction. The problem is, I want that human interaction to meet my intangible longings.

> *"When I was a child, I spoke like a child, I thought like a child, I reasoned like a child. When I became a man, I gave up childish ways. For now we see in a mirror dimly, But then face to face. Now I know in part; then I shall know fully, even as I have been fully known."*
> —1 Corinthians 13:11–12

This is a fork in the road. And it's one I've met more than a few times. I want God here and now, not later. I don't want to *see in a mirror dimly.* I want to see *face to face*—now. And to the degree that I indulge that understandable angst, I will erect gods to pacify. I will elevate all manner of things or people or pursuits in the hopes they will touch the longing. I will begin the construction of an earthly home and dull the forthcoming inner discord. I will pretend.

Or I can go back to the fork in the road and choose the other way. It's far less traveled, but as I allow my faith to exercise itself, I will soon discover this is the road I was made to travel on. It is the right road, but not because it is easy to traverse. *"Enter by the narrow gate. For the gate is wide and the way is easy that leads to destruction, and those who enter by it are many. For the gate is narrow and the way is hard that leads to life, and those who find it are few"* (Matt. 7:13–14).

There is nothing whatsoever lovely about the experience a baby has as he or she moves through the daunting birth canal, yet there is no question that the baby is traveling via the only natural port of entrance into the world. That kind of angst is mine, too, as I move along the right path, in fellowship with God. I experience both *now* and *not yet*. God prepares for my homecoming *and* has made His home in me now. As narrow as the life-gate might be, and as arduous as the path often is, I experience *home* with God as I remain on it. I have never settled for a lesser version of life when I have traveled the narrow road. It has been and remains the fulfillment of my greatest dream, even with a persistent presence of hardship.

There are two thick strands that make my occupation of the fourth chair a true homecoming. They make up the bulk of why I believe there is no other true home than the one found in the company of God:

"The heavens declare the glory of God, And the sky above proclaims His handiwork."
—Psalm 19:1

"I praise You, for I am fearfully and wonderfully made. Wonderful are Your works; my soul knows it very well."
—Psalm 139:14

"For His invisible attributes, namely, His eternal power and divine nature, have been clearly perceived, ever since the creation of the world, in the things that have been made..."
—Romans 1:20

"So God created man [mankind] *in His own image..."*
—Genesis 1:27

If God made all that exists, and if His invisible attributes are seen in the things He's made, then all that exists teaches us something about the nature of God. All that's been made has an imprint of the Living God on it and in it. But not everything God has made bears the *same* imprint. The Creation narrative in Genesis chapter 1 lets us know that, unique to all the other created order, God made humans in His image.

I bear an image of God. All humans do. But each of us bears His image uniquely as we are each uniquely created. There is no one like me. There never has been and never will be, though billions of humans bookend me on the timeline. It follows, then, that within me is a signature of God unlike any other signature, so that you could only collect this particular bit of information about God as you saw it reflected in me. No one else could reflect it because no one else bears it. Only I do.

The realization of my unique *signature* establishes, in part, the validity of my occupation of the fourth chair as a sort of homecoming. Where else could I be more at home than in the company of the One whose image I bear? Who else would I be more known and understood by than my Creator? Why would God make me uniquely and then NOT seek me out to be in fellowship with Him?

We are all sought after. We are all invited to come home. We recognize the imprint of God on us, and we grab hold of the gift of life offered us through Jesus Christ. When we exercise our faith in Christ, we yield to His kingship and relinquish our will to His. As that transaction takes place, we are given a place within His family.

Paul's letter to the church in Ephesus begins with these life altering words. I encourage you to read this passage very slowly, letting each phrase settle before you read the next: *"Blessed be the God and Father of our Lord Jesus Christ, who has blessed us in Christ with every spiritual blessing in the heavenly places, even as He chose us in Him before the foundation of the world, that we should be holy and blameless before Him. In love He predestined us for adoption to Himself as sons through Jesus Christ, according to the purpose of His will, to the praise of His glorious grace, with which He has blessed us in the Beloved. In Him we have redemption through His blood, the forgiveness of our trespasses, according to the riches of His grace, which He lavished upon us, in all wisdom and insight making known to us the mystery of His will, according to His purpose, which He set forth in Christ as a plan for the fullness of time, to unite all things in Him, things in heaven and things on earth"* (Eph. 1:3–10).

The implications of what Paul was telling the Ephesians can't be overemphasized. It is truth that reaches through time to you and me. There is a grand plan in place, conceived by God from eternity. In Christ I can be united with God. In Christ I can become part of the family of God. The moment that happens, I am made new. I am no longer who I was but have become who I was always made to be. I enter the family of God. My adoption into that family comes with all the rights and benefits...as if I were *"begotten of the Father"* (John 1:14).

> *"For as many as are led by the Spirit of God, these are sons of God. For you did not receive the spirit of bondage again to fear, but you received the Spirit of adoption by whom we cry out, "Abba, Father." The Spirit Himself bears witness with our spirit that we are children of God, and if children, then heirs—heirs of God and joint*

heirs with Christ, if indeed we suffer with Him,
that we may also be glorified together."
—Roman 8:14–17, NKJV

And so with this sonship, I find myself not only an image bearer but a daughter, having a "spiritual DNA" that validates or substantiates my place in the family of God. I take my place in His company, and there, I am at home. There is no substitute for the intimacy and synchronicity I share with God. The fellowship—the experience of family that I have within the body of Christ, becomes meaningful when it functions as a natural extension of what I enjoy with God. And I have something that's indispensable to contribute to my spiritual siblings that comes out of the overflow of meaningful relationship with God. If there is no substance in my personal experience of God, there won't be anything substantial for me to offer the rest of my family. And in that case, the experience of home will have all the hallmarks of dysfunction I find outside the family of God.

I have, for about forty years now, enjoyed a visceral experience with God as I sit at my piano and play. It is such a highly personal activity for me, even though most often, I'm playing in front of people, leading them in worship. But even as I quietly play, or play and sing at home in the privacy of my office, I'm overwhelmed by the gift of His engaging presence. He is with me and seems eager that I know it. Almost without exception, whether I'm in a stadium full of people, in front of my precious church community, leading at a conference somewhere, or at home alone, I feel entirely safe and insulated. My surroundings fade, and I lean in His direction, trusting Him to multiply my offering to Him so those in the room can enter. My husband calls that being a lead worshipper, rather than being the worship leader. It makes for a supernatural environment that others can use as a means to express their own hearts before the Lord. It's all driven by the Holy Spirit, and it's life-giving to anyone who would enter.

I am very much at home and at rest as I worship God with music. I've always relished a setting that, by design, requires my full attention be on God, where the best I possess is able to flow freely in His direction. And He has proven the most attentive companion, receiving my worship while tending to the needs of my heart.

In the years of late, as I have practiced occupying my chair, I have come to find that same sense of rest and companionship popping up in bits of my life that, up until then, most often were sources of unrest. He is teaching me that He can be found, and intends to be found, in the full spectrum of my life. Every scenario in the course of a day provides an opportunity to remember He is there, to engage Him, to ascribe worth to Him, to invite His Spirit to speak or move or instruct or advise. And because I am at home with Him, wherever GPS says I am, I can and do experience that same sense of enveloping companionship.

I have come to know the companionship of God steady me in all manner of life experiences. I am realizing a quality of life with Him that I would scarcely have dreamt possible. He is attentive. He is accepting. He is kind and exceedingly patient. He is always there for me. Always.

The quality of His companionship has deeply impacted my own heart toward other people. I'm quicker to identify and come alongside someone in pain. I'm quicker to remember there is a longing heart at the core of even the angriest person. And when my heart is tempted to self-protect or respond harshly, those occupying the other three chairs in my company remind me that we do not hate; we build up. We do not tear down; we support and encourage. We are not impatient; we are long-suffering with one another. We create and maintain a safe space for people to be authentically themselves and spur them on to become all they are meant to be. We set a place for them at the table and then feed their hungry souls out of the abundance of the fruit produced by the Holy Spirit in us. We prepare a room especially for them, and then we open the door and call them to come home, just like God has done for us.

> *God, it seems You've been our home forever; long before the mountains were born, Long before You brought earth itself to birth, from "once upon a time" to "kingdom come"—You are God.*
> —Psalm 90:1–2, MSG

Chapter 10

Anchored
The Reliability of His Company

*"We have this as a sure and steadfast anchor of
the soul, a hope that enters into the inner place
behind the curtain."*
—Hebrews 6:19

*"For they call themselves after the holy city, and
stay [anchor] themselves on the God of Israel; the
LORD of hosts is His name."*
—Isaiah 48:2

I have attached my soul to God. The author of the book
of Hebrews used the metaphor of an anchor to describe
this attachment. The obvious picture is of a ship securing
itself to something that will keep it in place so it does
not drift. The attachment is made via an anchor that
derives from the ship. The entire success of the arrangement is predicated on the reliability of what the anchor
is attached to. If that attachment fails, the ship and the
anchor are set adrift.

According to the passage in the sixth chapter of

Hebrews, my soul has a metaphoric anchor fixed to it, an extension of my soul that is, by design, meant to make a secure connection with something beyond itself. In this passage of Scripture, the anchor is called "hope," and hope has secured itself to the promises God has made to His children.

In Paul's letter to the Church of the Thessalonians, he encourages and affirms these Christ followers for their *"labor of love and steadfastness of hope in our Lord Jesus Christ"* (1 Thess. 1:3). He is implying there is a steadfastness to this anchoring in Christ.

So I hope in our *Lord Jesus Christ* and in the things God promises. I have an expectation or anticipation that God is a promise keeper and is Himself reliable. I hope in Him. Without question, the Bible lets me know that this anchoring of my soul is something I am to have, hold fast to, and be able to give language to.

> *"So when God desired to show more convincingly to the heirs of the promise the unchangeable character of His purpose, He guaranteed it with an oath, so that by two unchangeable things, in which it is impossible for God to lie, we who have fled for refuge might have strong encouragement to hold fast to the hope set before us. We have this as a sure and steadfast anchor of the soul, a hope that enters into the inner place behind the curtain, where Jesus has gone as a forerunner on our behalf..."*
> —Hebrews 6:17–20

> *"In your hearts honor Christ the Lord as holy, always being prepared to make a defense to*

anyone who asks you for a reason for the hope
that is in you…"
—1 Peter 3:15

When I am anchored to God, my soul is secure because the Source of my attachment cannot falter. The Triune God cannot fail in any measure. Whatever transpires within their company is entirely reliable. That is a reality utterly foreign to humans who are obviously accustomed to engaging with other humans. We anchor to one another in varying measures. We place our hope in those we have attached ourselves to. And of course, we fail one another because we do not have the capacity to relate to anyone flawlessly. God has to teach me, as I learn what it is like to be in relationship with Him, that it will not be like any other association.

Plainly stated, when I anchor to God, I am one human anchoring her soul to the one true God. I overstate this because most of my disappointment with God, as it has to do with feeling secure in my anchoring to Him, happens because I forget that one of us is God. I forget that He is not human, but the Creator of humans. I forget that He does not think, or act, or plan, or execute plans like humans do. I have practically no idea the context in which He enters a situation. I am debilitatingly limited, and He is infinitely resourced. My wisdom leads to death (see Proverbs 14:12). God's wisdom is life and light (see Psalm 119:89–93). His wisdom is eternal and cannot fail (see Isaiah 40:8).

Do you remember ever asking someone if you could trust them? *"Can I trust you?"* That's a question that seeks to spotlight the quality of people's character so you know if you are safe with them. Have you ever found yourself asking God that question? "Can I trust You, God?" I have. I've no idea, other than I was not struck with lightning, how the question went over with Him.

I've had a difficult time remembering that my trust or lack of trust in His reliability has nothing at all to do with His reliability! When I trust Him, He is altogether trustworthy. When I do not trust Him, He remains altogether trustworthy. What He says He will do, He will do. It's most often not going to happen like I would like for it to, but it's going to happen just as God has planned. He's not going to skip even one detail in carrying out His promises.

It's a strange thing to come to terms with the fact that while God never changes, my level of trust in Him seems to have an overactive sliding scale that can only ever be attributed to a misapplication of the scale. I'm accustomed to using my mental scale to move toward other people responsibly. But no scale should ever come anywhere near the living God.

Practicing trusting God has been a far greater feat than I imagined it would be. I'm the X factor because I have only ever found Him trustworthy. Never has there been a reason for me to find Him anything but reliable. Still, too often when I could trust Him, I don't. I rely on myself. If I ever paused to ask myself who I found more reliable, God or me, I wouldn't hesitate to place myself in God's hands. But rarely will a day go by that I don't still show my propensity for self-reliance.

Each morning, I ask the Lord to manage the pieces of my day—to be the One who sets the schedule and the pace of the day. But here and there, I still find myself interjecting bits of my own to-do list. Part of that is just me being lazy. It feels expedient sometimes to circumvent

His counsel and do what I want in the moment. But I sometimes sense His clear leading and choose to push back against it, especially if it doesn't make sense to me. The truth is, God may ask you and I to do things that seems a little crazy, or even a lot crazy.

There is a scene in *The Chosen* (season one, episode seven), a drama about the life of Jesus, in which the writers take the audience back to the time of Moses. Joshua is watching Moses fashion a bronze serpent that God told him to make. Joshua is indignant that Moses is crafting this "pagan" image rather than doing something practical to aid the people who are dying from snake bites (see Numbers chapter 21). Joshua is questioning whether or not Moses heard the Lord correctly, and Moses replies very simply, "I have learned to do what He says without questioning Him." That is a line of fiction written by the screenwriter, but there's no question that Moses grew to trust the Lord in just that way.

The idea that I would do what God says without questioning Him implies I would have questions. Most likely, there are going to be things about the instructions the Lord gives me that will elicit questions. But those questions are not supposed to act as barriers on my path to obedience. Moses gives me hope that I can grow in my trust of God. And God continues to patiently teach me to practice trusting Him.

In this particular season of my life, I've sometimes sensed the Lord saying to me, "Anne, One of us is God. Have you possibly forgotten? You're hesitant to trust Me. You know that only trouble can come from that, don't you?"

And my spirit answers Him, "I know. Sorry. I really don't have a good explanation. Help, Lord!"

I am ever-endowed with the freedom to choose to trust God or not. It's one thing to say I trust Him, but unless that bears itself out through my willingness to cooperate fully, I'm *not* yet trusting.

How long do you imagine it takes for a child of God to learn to hold fast to the hope set before him or her—to remain in the safety and certainty of the fourth chair? This lifelong endeavor is a picture of trusting in God's perfect ability to manage all things pertaining to my life. But it also means I practice the giving over of my will. I might trust God but simply want to exercise my own will. I've had versions of this conversation with God before:

Anne: God, I trust You, but I don't really want You involved in the situation with so-and-so. I'll handle it. I know what You would do...so don't worry. I've got this.

God: So, you're asking me to stay out of it? I want us both to be clear.

Anne: Well, technically I guess I'm asking you not to get involved. Of course I trust You, but I've got this.

God: [*Crickets.*]

I can run the show of my life myself, or I can submit to God's pervasive influence. But I can't do both. By remaining in the fourth chair, I remain in the company of my Chief Advocate and Advisor. I posture myself to listen and respond affirmatively to whatever I might hear in His company. I practice trust, understanding "one of us is God." I then begin to thrive as I lay aside my will and submit to His. I settle in and embrace my chief purpose in life—to bring glory to God and to offer life and love to other people. I experience the Spirit of God directing and empowering me. My soul is at ease—entirely safe, even in the face of the harsh realities of being alive in this day and age. I live sure-footed…steady, certain that the One I'm anchored to is and will forever be immovable. And I know the pleasure of companionship with God because I finally live in harmony with Him.

For me, there is no more effective classroom to practice learning to trust than in a difficult, familiar situation in which I have largely failed to trust the Lord's leading. I would *much* prefer to learn in a new setting altogether, but if breakthrough happens within a context of repeated personal failure, the roots of my trust in God go so much deeper. It is a glorious thing to look back and bear witness to God's deliverance in an area of chronic hardship.

Covenant relationship provides a pretty amazing context to learn the art of submission to God. That's a prime environment for God to carve away at me-centeredness. My husband and I are approaching our thirty-third anniversary. We would both tell you that God has used our marital conflicts to help us practice trusting Him. Those areas within our relationship where John and I simply could not seem to gain any ground were genuine sources of frustration, especially because we knew that each of us was trying our best to understand the other person. So we began to practice taking those issues into our respective fourth chairs together. We set aside a place in our home and met together every day. We weren't there to talk to each other about issues, but to talk to God. We began to open our hearts as honestly as we knew how to in the company of God and one another. We put our problem-solving skills on hold and practiced laying our issues down in the light of God's presence. Once that happened and the burden of solving problems was set aside, we were in a position to really hear from the Lord. We weren't trying to use God as a sounding board to air out our frustrations. We truly needed to hear from Him.

For quite some time, it did not seem like the Lord addressed the frustrations that John and I held at all. He did not seem concerned about them as much as He was determined for us to rediscover each other's heart. We had stopped *seeing* one another. Instead, when we looked at each other, we saw disputes between us. Neither of us was aware of this until we sat together a while in the presence of God. When we began to hear one another cry out to the Lord, we saw past the issues and right into the depth of each other's heart. It was an experience we were not prepared for. The Lord broke our hearts for each other, and nothing after was ever the same.

John and I had put ourselves in a position to *have* to be willing to be vulnerable, honest, and humble. We were side by side, each in our fourth chair and in the presence of the Triune God. We had to trust God with our raw hearts and die to any personal agenda. We had to put ourselves in a position to have to embrace whatever God would say to us.

I can't tell you how many times I used to move toward the Lord to articulate a grievance (whether in my marriage, parenting, or at work), so certain that God would be in agreement with *my* position. My ultimate objective was not to preserve or protect relationship as much as to solve a long-standing dispute. Because of that, I frequently found myself under the conviction of the

Holy Spirit. Too often, John and I would bring things to Him in the hopes of finding an ally rather than seeking relational wholeness.

That's not to say God did not address those disputes. He met us and helped us work through all kinds of things. But He did it when it was time, according to Him. We have waited moments for answers. We have waited decades for answers. Regardless of when or how they came, as children of God anchored in His presence, our job was to practice trusting Him and yielding to His leadership. To say He took amazing care of both of us, is to understate the impact of His pervasive care. I don't have language to do Him justice. But He was beyond amazing.

As the Spirit of God keeps on teaching me to remain in my chair—to rely on the anchor of my soul attached to Him, I have been learning not to fear those times when I do not "feel" anchored. There are more times than I'm comfortable with, when I do not feel and sense Him. These are different kinds of moments that expose the quality of my trust in Him. Is He there when I don't feel Him there? Is He not simply present but taking an active role, even when I'm not aware of Him? When the tether between the edge of my soul and the anchor in Him is slack, do I *feel* adrift? Do I know for certain I am still firmly anchored, even when my feelings try to tell me differently?

One of the reasons I have left the fourth chair has been a reaction to the sensation that I am adrift. The feeling of being unsafe or alone can send me into a spin. In years gone by, I would be darting in and out of His company daily. I was constantly usurping the control I had yielded to God and applying my own inferior reasoning. I was trying to position myself so that I would feel as if I had my feet under me. And all that effort was fruitless. Eventually, I experienced a season of life when I was, in effect, unable to move myself at all.

For about six years, flying on an airplane was very traumatic for me. Every aspect of travel was a source of a potential panic attack. Because most of the work my husband and I did required an airplane (or three) to deliver us to our temporary workplace (then one or three flights to get home), this became an ongoing, significant life issue. I never used to give a thought to any aspect of travel. I enjoyed it as much as I enjoyed the work we did once we arrived where we were going. But then I became fearful and hyperattentive to every detail of a trip, including the planning stages.

The old Anne would have been happy to learn about the trip as it unfolded. The new me was obsessed far in advance of a trip, needing to know the routing we'd take, the time of day we would leave, the seat I had on the plane, the time between segments of flight, and on and on. I was fighting panic at the thought of an upcoming trip. I was deep breathing during the days preceding a trip and then trying to remain calm on travel day. What on Earth was happening to me? We did more international travel in those days than domestic. That meant a panic attack could span as much as thirty-six hours because that is how long it would take to get where we were going.

I did not understand panic attacks back then. I did not understand what was happening to me, let alone *why* it was happening. But God did. As arduous as those years were, God tended to me faithfully, during every segment of every itinerary. But I almost never felt it. I felt entirely adrift. My husband was extremely attentive and accommodating, but I still felt utterly alone.

Most of the time during the trip, my mind was able to acknowledge the reality of God's presence, but sometimes not. God *was* present, and I *was* safe and secure, even without the felt sense of it. My anchor held through years of intense suffering. My anchor held because God cannot fail. It was both terrible and wondrous to have undergone those years of panic attacks. Because of it, the truth that I am secure in the capable, protective embrace of God now informs moments that used to be excruciating. He generously sustained my family and me through those years of hardship.

At my core (at everyone's core) is a desire to find a person I can place my trust in. I instinctively understand that person would have to be a superhuman. And I need that person to possess unlimited resources, unlimited knowledge, and unlimited power. This would ensure that my fragile self would remain safely anchored, no matter what.

Deeper still, underneath these implausible scenarios, is the need for this superhuman to love me. And the person's capacity for love would need to be unlimited and unchanging. Why? Because only then could I truly open myself up to that person's comprehensive control of my life. It would be this person's love for me that would be the compelling factor in my surrender.

In the magnificent three Persons of the Trinity, I find all these attributes. They share them even as they share one another's essence. Every characteristic is found in its fullness in each of the Persons of God. I find in God a nature that is eternal and never changing, as Jesus's brother, James. Stated: *"With whom there is no variation or shadow due to change"* (James 1:17).

When I anchor to God and occupy my place in His presence, I have secured myself to One whose heart toward me is only good, only loving, only loyal, and fiercely protective—One who has the desire and ability to conform me in to the likeness of Christ, for His glory. It's here that I am fully known and eternally, extravagantly loved. I can find this nowhere else. I can find this with no other person on Earth. It has been God's objective all along that I not only learn of His trustworthiness, but that I would live it out through a life of singular devotion to Him.

Oswald Chambers has some powerful words to offer regarding God's utter reliability and the fact that it is found nowhere else:

> There is only one Being Who can satisfy the last aching abyss of the human heart, and that is the Lord Jesus Christ. Why Our Lord is apparently so severe regarding every human relationship is because He knows that every relationship not based on loyalty to Himself will end in disaster.[1]

I would add that we would also despair of ourselves.

I have a sure and steadfast *anchor of the soul.* His name is I Am. I trust in Him, and that trust launches and fuels the relationships I have with other people. I am anchored. I am home with God, in the fourth chair—known and loved and safe. His utter reliability brings a steadiness and peace to my soul, whether the day brings calm or chaos.

---

1. Oswald Chambers, "My Utmost for His Highest," Utmost website, https://utmost.org/classic/the-discipline-of-disillusionment-classic/.

"When darkness veils His lovely face,
I rest on His unchanging grace;
In every high and stormy gale,
My anchor holds within the veil.

On Christ, the solid Rock, I stand;
All other ground is sinking sand,
All other ground is sinking sand."
—"The Solid Rock," a hymn written by Edward Mote
in 1834

Chapter 11

Hope Filled
Living Life from the Fourth Chair

"Hope deferred makes the heart sick, but a desire fulfilled is a tree of life."
—Proverbs 13:12

"For you, O Lord, are my hope, my trust, O Lord, from my youth."
—Psalm 71:5

"The steadfast love of the Lord never ceases, His mercies never come to an end; they are new every morning; great is Your faithfulness. 'The LORD is my portion,' says my soul, 'therefore I will hope in Him.'"
—Lamentations 3:22–24

"I hope so." That's a phrase I've used countless times in my life. It describes a desire for something to come to pass, but confesses at least a measure of reluctance to believe it will. That is *not at all* how the word "hope" is introduced in the Old and New Testaments. Hope articulates something I am sure about. "I hope" is synonymous with, "I expect" or "I'm certain." This is a crucial differentiation to make right at the top of a chapter titled "Hope Filled."

To occupy my place in the company of God is to experience a hope-filled life. So, what might it mean to be hope-filled? It's another way of asking what it means to live from the fourth chair. Our modern dictionaries define "hope" *as a feeling of expectation and desire for a certain thing to happen.* But as a Christ follower I have a critical addition to make to that definition. It's the difference between hoping with my fingers crossed and hoping with patience, assurance, and joy.

It is God, the singular object of my hope, who transforms the way the word "hope" lives in me. Hope is a picture of the anchor of my soul attached to God, and because of the unfailing nature of God, I am entirely secure in that attachment to Him. I could rightly say that hope is the expectation that God will always and only ever be Himself. I could hope for nothing more than that!

When my dear friend was in the throes of grief after losing her husband in the prime of his life, she honestly did not know how she would live through that day, or any of the subsequent days. This went on for many, many months. She was not necessarily despairing. She was not without hope. She was, however, so profoundly stricken with grief that she could not imagine surviving it. She had been cast into the most undulant, violent sea, but she was anchored to God, and she trusted the anchor would not fail. That's a powerful picture of living a hope-filled life.

I needed help from the Lord in understanding what it meant to be filled with hope. Like almost every illumination from the Spirit, those surrounding the word "hope" began with the dismantling of my limited understanding, followed by a fresh, accurate introduction to hope. It meant I was soon to have a new way of thinking about hope. With hope newly defined, I started looking for evidence of hope in my daily life. I was practicing the new things I learned.

I was going to be looking for a visceral sense of hope in situations where previously I'd felt hopeless. God "walked me around the word" so I could get a better look at it, and then He cleaned my glasses so I could see what was in front of me. Hope had always been there because God had always been there. I was getting my first really good look at it...at *Him*. Even at first glance, hope started to do what hope does...it was igniting my heart. It was calling me to expectant living.

It's easy, even instinctive, to attach hope to getting the job you really want or being asked out on a date by a person you are attracted to. It's easy to anchor hope to your preferred presidential candidate being elected, or the latest vaccine hitting the market, or a breakthrough in your marriage, or finally conquering an addiction, or having law and order restored on the streets of cities all over America.

These are good desires and worthy pursuits. But my hope belongs in the hands of God alone. Then the outcomes of those worthy pursuits don't have undo power to control me. God is trustworthy, so regardless of the outcome of any life circumstance, hope remains. That doesn't mean we don't peacefully protest when God calls us to do that. It doesn't mean we don't run for office in our town or state to bring needed change. But if we do those things, we never unpin our hope on God and attach it to the *outcome* of our pursuits.

At this point in my life, I live as a woman of hope, and I have done so for many years now. Prior to that, hope would surface but wane easily. I was a woman whose hope was nearly exclusively pinned to what would come after this life. I practiced keeping my head down and thinking ahead to what was coming, but that meant I was not living my day-to-day life with hope. I was not living with a sense of expectancy up and until I would go home to be with Jesus. I was *enduring* life rather than *embracing* that sense of anticipation that because God was present, something amazing could happen at any moment.

But all that changed when I settled in the fourth chair. My possession of the fourth chair is far from theoretical. It's not an image I conjure up and practice "seeing." It describes the reality that I live in communion/community with God. And maybe that description provides *the* key insight into my former lack of hopefulness. I had lost a sense of purpose and instead committed to embracing a set of principles.

The Lord opened my eyes to the relational life with Him I was missing out on. His companionship is quite literally the reason I now live hope-filled. I live with an ever-present expectation of encountering Him and engaging with Him. The way the details of my life play out is entirely secondary. It doesn't mean they are not important. It does mean they are not of primary importance.

For instance, instead of thinking about the things I knew about God as I was boarding a plane (which was like entering a coffin during my years of extreme panic), I began to listen for Him in the quiet of my heart. There I could hear God whisper that He was present, and I practiced adjusting to that truth. It changed everything about the moments I found myself in. How could it not? As I slipped into my seat on the plane, I knew I was also in the fourth chair. I was far from alone as the panic was looking for a place in me to take hold. My focus shifted from my environment and the invitation to panic to the presence of my companion. In my spirit, I heard the Lord say, "Look at me, Anne. Remember—I'm God. I'm beside you, and I'm not leaving. My presence changes everything about this moment for you. It's safe for you to hope in Me." And over a bit of time, as the panic persisted but had no place to take hold, it stopped coming altogether.

What was happening to me? Why was a circumstance that had not outwardly changed in any way ceasing to elicit the debilitating response it used to? How was I OK when I used to be anything but OK? God was teaching me to look at Him every minute of every day and night, no matter where I was, no matter what was taking place: "Look at me, Anne. Remember, I'm God. I'm beside you, and I'm not leaving. It's safe for you to hope in Me."

The miraculous began showing up in every aspect of my life, including my marriage. Those bits that John and I couldn't seem to navigate in our relationship with each other began to look very different to both of us as we shifted our hope off the other spouse "finally getting it" and on to Jesus. It was starting to be enough that He was there and at work, however He decided to work. We had to choose not to fix our expectations about how an issue was going to resolve but on the Lord having His way. Personal agendas had to fade entirely. We had to practice choosing to place our hope in God. Whatever victory looked like to Him, that's what we were interested in seeing happen. We were hoping in Him. How liberating!

Maybe the most beautiful and unexpected by-product of hope, rightly placed, is that John and I once again found ourselves positioned side by side as we approached conflicts that had put us in opposite camps through failure to make headway. Those adversarial emotions that arise when you can't agree on how to load a dishwasher, let alone how to navigate the giant pieces of life, can too easily leave you embittered toward the person you love.

When true hope comes, you experience the melting away of bitterness and the renewal of compassion and tenderness. You begin to fight *for* one another rather than *against* each other. You begin to live your life Christ-centered and hope-filled, not because you're going to see every conflict magically disappear, because you won't. But God begins to orient you to something far more important than having your issues resolved. He begins to capture your attention with Himself. And when you are looking at Him—paying attention to Him (which means you are no longer paying attention to yourself), the order of the priorities of life fall into place. There is something down deep inside the soul that recognizes this is right-side-up living, and you begin to breathe deep sighs of relief.

When I truly began to settle in to the fourth chair, and when I pressed in to my Companion, asking Him daily (hourly) to keep my eyes fixed on Him and nowhere else, there was no aspect of daily life that remained untouched by that awareness. Nothing was so small that it became incidental as I laid eyes on it from the fourth chair. Nor was there anything so insurmountable that God could not intervene and do whatever it suited Him to do. Whether or not God would intervene or insert Himself was no longer my primary concern. He was my concern. I began to practice trusting Him to be God, reminding myself that my thoughts are not His thoughts. My ways are not His ways.

This was like having a deep spiritual cleansing. There came a vividness to every action, every object my eyes fell on, every encounter with another human being—each moment had an import, as it should, as if something transcendent might happen. And of course, because God is present and active, the supernatural is always melding with the natural. Remember Elijah's prayer for Elisha? *"So the LORD opened the eyes of the young man* [Elisha]*, and he saw, and behold, the mountain was full of horses and chariots of fire all around Elisha"* (2 Kings 6:17).

I felt free. I *was* free and had been a free woman for decades, but I had barely dipped into the pool of freedom. I was now living, actually freely living, my life in the constant company of God. I was experiencing the sureness of anchoring to God, and hope was alive in me because God was alive in me.

Romans chapter 5 reminds me that hope is a product of character building—that as God has His way in me, and the likeness of Christ is being formed in me, I grow as a woman of character. As character grows, hope is produced. So I could be free and not initially have the experience of all the fullness of free living. That concept is familiar to Christians. We come into the fullness of what God has given to us progressively. Children grow into their potential. Employees grow in competency in their positions at work. Husbands and wives grow into their roles as married people. And children of God grow in maturity and hope as they grow in relationship with God.

My friend was in a serious car accident recently. She sits very deeply with the Lord and is a woman of prayer. In the months following her accident, she suffered from significant fear whenever she drove, especially as flashbacks from the accident would come. She had been seeking God faithfully to meet her since the accident, but as we were talking one day, she realized she had not dialogued with God specifically about the growing fear. Would God want to be invited in to that part of the aftermath of her experience? Would He want to intervene and meet her at the point of that fear? Of course He would, and my friend knew it. So in that moment of realization, she began a dialogue with God. She offered her fear to Him, knowing He was willing to come and meet her. God immediately dissolved her fear, eager to interject Himself into that very specific detail of her life.

That was a good reminder for me, that while I speak to God about things in general, I can't forget He's walking beside me in real time. The subtleties tucked in my day are meant to be shared with Him, too. That's a big part of hope-filled living. Sometimes I still forget He's beside me. Doesn't that seem impossible? When I come to my senses, I remind myself, "Anne, God is right beside you. How are you not aware of Him?" And then I feel my spirit sheepishly turn to Him and say, "Hi. I see You now. I actually forgot You were here. No good explanation for how a person could forget God is present. Ugh. Thanks for Your patience—again!" I never feel the slightest condemnation in those moments—only love and acceptance.

It was good that I was growing in my awareness of Him. It was good that I was acknowledging Him and then yielding to Him. It was good I was practicing setting aside my agenda and asking Him to do what was right in His eyes. But I was still one critical step short of experiencing all it meant to belong to Him.

There's nothing necessarily personal in an arrangement where God is seen and invited to essentially manage details. That's a utilitarian arrangement that my heart doesn't even need to show up for.

The American economy hits the skids when the stock market crashed in 2008. With that economic nose dive, corporations starting to pull benefit packages away from their employees to cut costs. Bonuses were being pulled, and that extra lump sum at the end of year wasn't going to be paid out anymore. Employees were irate, and I felt indignant on their behalf. Then I had a long talk with a mentor whose spent his carrier in upper corporate management. He asked me if I could define what I thought a benefits package was, what a bonus was. As I began to state the obvious, I was realizing what he meant for me to clue in to. People were so accustomed to bonuses, etc. they had structured their personal finances to *depend* on receiving them. When the bonuses stopped coming, many portfolios were devastated.

I believe I viewed my relationship with God similarly. I built my life not around the relationship I entered with Him. It was the bonus package—what He could do *for* me that I hinged my heart to. He did not invite me to Himself so I could be provided for. He invited me Himself so I could know Him, so that He and I could commune together. His provision for me was part of an eternal benefits package, and while I could depend on it, He never meant it to act as a replacement for the devotion of my heart.

Too often, my heart would erupt with frustration at God for *not* coming through as I knew He could. For decades, this was a constant reality. I was over and over disappointed and disillusioned with God. My hope was fully invested in God doing what I needed God to do—what I knew He *could* do. Pinning my expectations on what God might do reduced God to a genie I could call into service. That was never going to be OK with God.

What I'm really trying to make my way to is this: it matters where my hope is fixed. It matters as much where my hope is *not* fixed. The word "hope" *has* to ultimately be reserved to describe my soul's anchoring to the three blessed persons of the Trinity. Any other application of the word "hope" is a grossly inferior use of the word, as in "I hope it rains tomorrow." There is nothing remotely similar about that innocuous statement than when I say, "I hope in God." I'm trying to practice reserving the word for Him. I've asked Him for other language to describe the lesser things I have expectations about.

The other day, I found myself in a situation with another person that I've been in more than a few times over the years, one that always comes with an engraved invitation to become bitter and resentful. This time I was conscious, while I was practically running to embrace resentment, that God was also present in that moment. He was offering me something entirely different. But what exactly was He offering me? Was He offering me a solution to the moment I was in? Was He offering to step in and fix something that needed fixing? What exactly was He there for, and how should I be feeling about His presence? An imaginary dialogue began between God and me:

Anne: I'm glad You're here.

God: I'm always here.

Anne: See this same ridiculous scenario with so-and-so? Of course You do. You're always here. It took zero seconds for my heart to get ugly about it! My heart is ugly! Now I have the thing with the person *and* an ugly heart.

God: Uh-huh.

Anne: You're here.

God: I am.

Anne: My hope is in You. It really is.

God: It really is.

Anne: So, how does hope work in a moment like this? If I'm hoping in You, what is it that I'm really hoping for? Maybe as usual, I've been thinking way too much about all the wrong things. How about if You just be You? How about in this aggravating moment, with my ugly heart, You be Yourself?

God: I can't be anyone other than Myself, so if that is what you're hanging your expectations on, you can hope with full assurance. I'm going to be Myself in this moment. I'm going to do God-stuff, as you say.

Anne: That's great. Seriously.

God: I'd like to ask *you* something now.

Anne: Fire away.

God: Anne? Look at Me. When this same aggravating thing happens again, if it happens again, look at Me and keep looking at Me. Expect Me to act like God because I actually am God. That will give Me the opportunity to place a different response in your heart, and at a minimum, you'll stop adding your ugliness to the pile. Leave all the rest to Me. Don't be offended if I say that the rest of this is not your business. It can't be both of our business. Keep your eyes on Me. Your hope in Me cannot fail.

Here is what strikes me maybe more deeply than any other aspect of the hope I have in God. I'm meant to live the whole of my life experiencing His companionship. That is what it means to live filled with hope. I occupy the fourth chair and enter the mysterious, reciprocal, eternal relationship God is enjoying within Himself. Communing with Him becomes an overwhelming source of joy. In this sacred fellowship, I give and receive love. My Triune God becomes the center of my focus and the object of my heart's devotion. In the presence of the fullness of God, I find sanctuary and companionship. I abide in the midst of the source of all wisdom and power and love. I am never alone, and I am never ever without hope.

> *"Therefore, since we have been justified by faith,*
> *we have peace with God through our Lord Jesus*
> *Christ. Through Him we have also obtained*
> *access by faith into this grace in which we stand,*
> *and we rejoice in hope of the glory of God.*
> *Not only that, but we rejoice in our sufferings,*
> *knowing that suffering produces endurance,*
> *and endurance produces character, and charac-*

ter produces hope, and hope does not put us to shame, because God's love has been poured into our hearts through the Holy Spirit who has been given to us."
—Romans 5:1–5

Chapter 12

Come and Live
Life in the Light of God's Presence

"Be to me a rock of refuge
to which I may continually come..."
—Psalm 71:3

"Come to Me,
all who labor and are heavy laden,
and I will give you rest.
Take My yoke upon you, and learn from Me,
for I am gentle and lowly in heart,
and you will find rest for your souls.
For My yoke is easy, and My burden is light."
—Matthew 11:28–30

In 1976,, Francis Schaeffer profiled our declining Western culture in his book *How Should We Then Live?* He gave language to what happens when we do not live in light of the literal existence of God or allow Him to influence the way we live. As Schaeffer traced the roots of our culture to ancient Rome (which took some of its cues from the Greeks) he said this:

> Like the Greeks, the Romans had no infinite god. This being so, they had no sufficient reference point intellectually; that is, they did not have anything big enough or permanent enough to which to relate either their thinking or their living. Consequently, their value system was not strong enough to bear the strains of life, either individual or political. All their gods put together could not give them a sufficient base for life, morals, values, and final decisions.[1]

The pages of this book have been giving language to what life can look like when a person is convinced of the reality of God, of His invitation to humans to engage with Him directly, and what can happen as a person heeds that invitation. If, as Schaffer suggests, all our gods put together cannot provide a sufficient system of belief for us to conduct our lives, then how good of God to alert us to His existence. How good of Him to reveal His desire to bring meaning and purpose to life by inviting us into His company through Jesus Christ. Plainly stated, He is not offering Himself as a viable option for living among all available options. He is revealing Himself as the *singular* path to life. All other paths come to an abrupt dead end. He is claiming, without hesitation or apology, that for me to choose any path other than the one into His presence is to choose death.

Humans have exercised their option to live independently of God from the beginning (remember Adam

---

1. The original version of the book was published by Francis A. Schaeffer: *How Should We Then Live? The Rise and Decline of Western Thought and Culture* (Ada, Michigan: Revell, 1976). This excerpt appears in the 2022 version, Francis A. Schaeffer, *How Should We Then Live? The Rise and Decline of Western Thought and Culture* (Wheaton, Illinois: Crossway, 2022), 18.

and Eve and the tree of the knowledge of good and evil). My flesh will never give up the fight to be the controlling force over the direction of my life. John Vianney, a Catholic Priest from the 1700s, offered this insightful observation: "God is like a mother who carries her child in her arms by the edge of a precipice. While she is seeking all the time to keep him from danger, he is doing his best to get into it." This is what humans do and have always done, rather than bow in submission and surrender to God.

Our flesh left to itself can do nothing else but exert its will toward independence. It would rather invent gods than submit to the Living God. But the moment we live as though we are independent beings, governed by our own wisdom, and under our own authority, we set out on a path that the Bible says, *"is the way to death"* (see Proverbs 14:12, 16:25).

Despite our age-old propensity for independence and disbelief, God invites us to come and live. *"Come, everyone who thirsts, come to the waters; and he who has no money, come, buy and eat! Come, buy wine and milk without money and without price. Why do you spend your money for that which is not bread, and your labor for that which does not satisfy? Listen diligently to Me, and eat what is good, and delight yourselves in rich food. Incline your ear, and come to Me; hear, that your soul may live; and I will make with you an everlasting covenant"* (Isa. 55:1–3). It is entirely beyond my comprehension that God offers this winsome invitation in light of the history of rebellion we've written, but He does.

"Come and live." This *is* an invitation. It is not an item to be purchased, yet to accept it requires the complete surrender of our souls. It means we will have to say no to the lie that we can be like God, capable of successfully self-governing. It means we will have to push past the delusion that the surrendering of our will is synonymous with locking ourselves within a prison cell. To self-govern ensures a life of bondage to sin, and ultimately to death. God's invitation into the fourth chair is an invitation into relationship that produces life and freedom at the cost of personal control. God is offering Himself, in the diversity of His three Persons: *"Come to Me; hear, that your soul may live"* (Isa. 55:3).

Living in light of the presence of God—occupying my place in the fourth chair—thoroughly transforms the entirety of my existence. It changes every thought, every emotion, every decision, every priority, every single thing I do and say for the rest of my life on this Earth. Like a drop of dye in a pitcher of water, it will make its way throughout until it thoroughly alters the contents. Chapter 10 of the Gospel of Mark recounts an event in Jesus's life when He was approached by a rich young man genuinely interested in following Him. When Jesus spelled out the breadth of what that would mean, the young man departed, not angry or defiant, but deeply grieved. He was not prepared or ultimately willing for the full contents of his life to be under Jesus's authority. All his sensibilities told him he must stay the course he was already on.

That young man would not have had any idea what he was actually being offered. The Living God was inviting him to follow and trying to rid him of encumbrances he would never experience in Jesus's company. He did not understand that Jesus was inviting him into true freedom and fulfillment, invaluable compared to the pleasure his wealth could provide him. He left the company of Jesus for the company of riches, two masters who never share those who serve them.

I live because of the love of God the Father, the wooing of the Spirit of God, and the gift offered through the work accomplished by the Son of God. I live in the company of this Triune God, and there, I am at home. God and I live as family, where He leads and I follow. Our family extends outward to include every other person throughout history who has accepted God's invitation to come and live. I have brothers and sisters too many to count. We are indispensable to one another, all called on to contribute to the health of our family as God has gifted us to do. We are meant to care for one another, to worship our God, and to bring light and hope to those outside our family. We do that in the hopes that they, too, would come and live. We love God and one another, each from our fourth chair.

It's impossible to be hopeless from the fourth chair—not because there is not debilitating hardship in this life, but because God will never stop being God. He will always be at work, tending to the most pertinent need, and doing so according to His perfect will. He does not promise that I will always see Him at work, but He expects me to trust that He is and to remain steadfast in the hope I have in Him. He does not promise I will understand what He is doing, but He reminds me continually that He does not think like I do. He asks and expects that I will stand strong in my assurance of who He is. He will never violate the covenant He has made with me or with any of His children. In fact, He has and will continue to fill in the gaps I create when I fail to keep covenant with Him. He waits only for me to reach for Him, repentant and submitted.

It's also impossible to see other human beings in the same way when I'm seated in the fourth chair. In fact, I am aware that I focus less and less on exterior circumstances people might create through their behavior. Instead, I'm trying to see the person behind the behavior. It changes every encounter with another person when I remind myself, "Anne, you're in the company of a human being uniquely created by God. Look past the trappings of his/her life. Look for the true heart underneath the exterior." I was not prepared for that shift to be the powerful and transforming experience it has been. And let me tell you, people notice. They know when you care enough to see them—*really* see them!

I see the troubled people in my life very differently, even when they have landed themselves in a mess. I used to focus on the mess and let that inform my response to the person. That is backwards in God's economy. Empowered by the Holy Spirit, I'm increasingly able to move toward that person with genuine compassion and hope. I move toward people as an agent of God who is longing to bring them the freedom they cannot procure for themselves. Do you know that people can tell immediately if I approach them fixated on their behavior and not on them? Do you know that chances are very good they feel far worse about their behavior than I do? If God is always intent on meeting with *me* at a heart level, how can I do less for others?

Life at home in the fourth chair has also transformed the way I move toward the people in my life who appear to have it all. God does not ever confuse the success a person might enjoy with the person behind the success. And when I am under His sway, neither do I. That is a great gift to be able to give to someone accustomed to being used because of his or her position in life. They, too, can despair of hope as people look past them to focus on what they might gain from an association with them. It's been helpful to check my heart and see what's produced in it as I approach the people of influence in my life. I want them to feel seen and safe.

From my fourth chair, I remember that the people in my life who are easy to be with and those who might be a little more challenging are all works in progress, as I am. Some of them are in relationship with God, and some are not. But each is an image bearer regardless, and for that reason they should be approached with dignity befitting an invaluable work of art, created by God. I must not unduly elevate any person over another. We are valued equally in the eyes of God, and my heart should reflect that fact. The Spirit of God in me sees right to the core of every person I encounter and invites me to engage with them behind their behavior. The Spirit does not confuse the heart of a person with his or her position, stature, or lack of either. He is always interested in reaching the soul. So, because the Spirit is in control of my life, I can exhibit that same consistency with people, regardless of their tendencies or temperaments.

None of those changes are possible, however, except and unless I'm occupying the fourth chair. The Triune God is the source of my hope, and He is the reason I see others differently. Nothing else matters if I don't get this right side up. The deepening of my relationship with God isn't possible *at all* unless the Spirit of God helps me. Any illumination I get about who He is will be credited to Him. Any deepening in my relationship with Him is credited to Him. I have to take my place in His company and open myself to Him. He is the Illuminator.

God is shaping and expanding my awareness of Himself and other people. He's doing that through my relationship with Him. He's meeting with me in the most personal way, most often as I open the Bible and wait on Him. God is cultivating within me a growing understanding of Himself as we do life together, using His Word as a primary, indispensable portal.

In the union I enjoy with God, the seen and the unseen worlds are always converging. My infinite God enters the finite space I occupy, and somehow my spirit enjoys the transcendent realm with His Holy Spirit. I experience home with Him, even while I wait to go home. He and I interrelate in every possible way as my day-to-day life unfolds. God and I are a "mobile" home, moving within a temporal world to which I am temporarily bound, but He is not.

All around me, the occupants of the unseen world are alive and active. Battles for the freedom of men and women are always being fought. I'm meant to be engaged in those battles for freedom as the Spirit of God directs me to be. It is an ongoing, intangible fact of life for anyone who occupies the fourth chair.

My God is the God of the seen, of all that is temporal. He is the God of all that exists in the unseen, of all that is eternal. He is Ruler over both realms, King of all. The constant convergence of the seen and unseen world is critical for me to keep in the fore of my mind. It is the larger story that brackets what I experience with my fleshly senses. What I perceive with my finite eyes is but a fragment of all that's taking place. My Companion helps me navigate, providing guidance and protection as I remain in the fourth chair.

God has invited me to *come and live*. He's eager for me

to thrive each day, even as I remember I am no longer of this world. As I grow more comfortable in His company, I grow increasingly uncomfortable in my temporary environment. God is teaching me to trust Him—to hinge all my expectations on Him, even as I navigate the systems of this world. I've had two devotionals published over the last few years. As I worked on the details of writing, costs, deadlines, etc., I had to fight the temptation to hinge my expectations on the success of those endeavors. God is teaching me to let *Him* use the systems the world has created, such as how a book gets published, but not attach my expectations there. It's far too easy to mis-attach.

Many days, I've sensed Him saying, "Anne, do what's in front of you today. Work on the bits of the book you need to, and make sure you apply yourself in a way that brings Me honor. But keep your eyes on Me. I'm in charge, and I have a plan. Don't get out ahead of me. Just do the day, and do it with integrity. And by the way, enjoy Me! If you miss that bit, you'll have missed the real gift I've set before you." I can do that from the fourth chair. I really can. I can trust Him and not get ahead of Him. I can apply myself with integrity to the work in front of me and still thoroughly enjoy His company.

When I'm in the fourth chair, my heart is very much alive. It's exposed and vulnerable—not to the world around me, but to Him. I'm in the support role in our relationship, taking my cues from Him. If I were His sous-chef, I would be prepping food for Him, in awe as I watched Him create culinary masterpieces. I would be wondering how on Earth I got to be the one to work at His side.

I am a redeemed human being in relationship with my

Creator. One of us is God! There is nothing at all of equal measure between us, yet I am never more myself than when I share His company. We enjoy a kind of friendship, but it's not like any other friendship. I'm learning to balance a genuine familiarity with Father, Son, and Spirit, with the awe and wonder that ought to accompany every moment in His company. That has been one of the greatest gifts of the picture of the four chairs. It's very hard to "see" them in my mind and not be struck by the incomprehensibility of my proximity to the Living God.

The highest experience you can have, even if you possessed all the riches of the universe and had the means to dispense those riches, is to commune with the King of kings. He is the windfall. I will have done you a massive disservice if you come away from reading this book with a "new perspective." My deepest prayer is that you would find *Him*, that you would know Him, and that you would not rest until you have made your way to His side and fixed yourself to Him. You and I do not need a revamped way to look at a system of belief. We need God. We need Father, Son, and Spirit. We need to come home and find the richness of the company He is offering us. Every single other aspect of what it means to be alive will fall into place if we come home and are content to stay home!

Look at these words from the apostle Paul. Look at what He counts as gain; it is *not* what you and I most often count as gain! *"Indeed, I count everything as loss because of the surpassing worth of knowing Christ Jesus my Lord. For His sake I have suffered the loss of all things and count them as rubbish, in order that I may gain Christ"* (Phil. 3:8). What do I count as having surpassing worth?

What would I gladly be rid of in order that I may gain Christ? The writer of Hebrews affirmed members of the early church as having *"joyfully accepted the plundering of your property, since you knew that you yourselves had a better possession and an abiding one"* (Hebr. 10:34). Part of my property is my mind and the freedom God gave me to make my own choices. Do I joyfully accept the plundering of that property—in order that I may gain Christ?

God invites me—and you—to *"come to Me and live."* When we look at something pure, like refined gold or a polished diamond, we are seeing something uncomplicated, and in that regard, it appears simplistic. But we don't forget the all-encompassing, arduous process of refinement necessary to reveal this treasure. Once we lay eyes on that treasure, we understand the tragedy it would be to stop before the process of refinement/purification is complete.

The Lord is refining me, and I am happy in Him. The Lord is purifying me, and I have only gained! There is nothing behind me I would go back to retrieve because it would mean I would not have Christ! He is everything.

If you were to open your Bible to Psalm 119 and linger there, you would discover the psalmist has been refined. He has achieved this refinement in the company of God through His Word. The psalmist's words reveal his deep love and passion for God. He speaks about the Word of God as if He's speaking about God Himself. And the language he uses is not unlike language you might reserve for a lover. He states emphatically that to love God (which he clearly does with his whole being) means he also loves what God loves. He is a man devoted to God's Word because His Word is an extension of Himself. He could not love God and not love His Word. *Note to self.*

God waits for us to find Him in the pages of His Word. We do not apply ourselves to the Word of God so that we might conquer the Holy Scriptures. Being in the Bible is not first an academic pursuit. We are looking for the One who saved us so we might commune with Him. Ask Him as you open His Word, "Tell me who You are. Tell me who I am. Tell me who we are as human beings." The Spirit of God, who dwells in you, will answer those questions. He longs for you to know.

I believe your biggest challenge will be, as mine is, to be patient, and then to be content with what He will say. He does not think like you and I do. His ways are not our ways. But He has never missed the mark in His work of refinement. He's never pulled the wrong syllabus off the shelf before He teaches. If He's speaking to you, listen! Trust that He's telling you just what you need to know and is delivering it to you at just the right time. Purpose to come to know Him as the psalmist did!

This morning, I was reading in the latter portion of the book of Exodus. Moses recounts how he used to go far outside the camp of the Israelites and pitch what he called "the tent of meeting." There, God would speak to him *"as a man speaks to his friend"* (Ex. 33:11). The people would stand at the entrance of their tents, inside the camp, and worship while Moses and God met together. Even as I marvel that God could speak to a human being in that intimate way, my heart breaks for the people inside the camp. I believe without doubt that God's intention was to meet with each of His people the way He was meeting with Moses.

Oh, that we would never settle for worshipping from afar, not when an invitation into the very presence of God has been extended. *"Come to Me and live."* He is asking for you by name. Father, Son, and Spirit wait for you to slip into the fourth chair and come home.

> *"And We will come to him and make Our home*
> *with him."*
> —John 14:23

Acknowledgments

I'm so very grateful to God for a simple metaphor of four chairs, occupied by Him and me, and for teaching me about the treasure of His companionship.

Thank you to my ever-faithful, loving husband, John, who supports me as I hold up in my office to write, study, and explore.

Thanks to my small but mighty band of blog readers who keep me accountable as I share developing thoughts.

Thank you to Joel Kilpatrick for encouraging me and for putting me on a particular agent's radar.

Thanks to my agent Greg Johnson at Wordserve Literary Agency for taking a chance on a middle-aged musician who loves to write. And, thank you for being particularly drawn to *The Fourth Chair* and asking me to write the book.

Thank you to Nadia Guy and the team at The Core Media Group, Inc. for your expertise and for seeing to it that this book has a chance to be read.

Special thanks to Donna Toney for your mentorship and support. And thank you to my dear friend Stacy

DeWitt for being a sounding-board for years of musings about the content of this and other books. I am rich in family, friends, and community. To God be the glory.

-Anne

About the Author

Anne Barbour has a unique lens on the world having spent over 30 years traveling and serving the ministries of Dr. Billy Graham, Franklin Graham, Greg Laurie and other Christian leaders. Those experiences have allowed her to witness up close the way Christian cultures all over the globe live out their faith. She has been active in the arena of contemporary worship as a singer and songwriter for 35 years, including developing and leading workshops, and ministering in churches and conference centers. Anne has authored three books and maintains a blog she describes as "musings and mutterings" about walking with God. Anne lives in Newbury Park, CA with her husband, John. They have one amazing son, along with his bride, and their grand puppy.

Other Books by Anne Barbour

The Savior Has Come

The Christmas narrative is a riveting one, yet it is one most of us file away until December rolls around. The coming of Jesus to the earth is a pivotal historic event that merits daily remembrance. Anne Barbour's The Savior Has Come will take you inside the events of the birth of Jesus, bringing the characters and places to life. Reading it will change your experience of Christmastime, and may just change your life as you revisit the significance of Jesus' arrival. Discover treasures hidden in plain sight in the story of the birth of Jesus. The Savior Has Come offers a unique reading format that is both refreshing and illuminating. Twenty-four Advent entries provide a simple, meaningful way to rediscover the familiar Biblical telling of the entrance of the Savior of the world. There are Biblical passages written in the text, reflections about the story, prayers, and a place for you to record thoughts and emotions. It was written for individual or group devotions and makes for a great first gift of Christmas.

Jesus | Love to the End

Is your experience leading up to Easter one filled with anticipation? It can be! Jesus Love to the End will help you saturate yourself in the story of Jesus' final weeks up and through His death and resurrection. As you do that, you will find yourself deeply appreciating Jesus and His radical display of love. There are Biblical passages written in the text, reflections about the story, prayers, and a place for you to record thoughts and emotions. Whatever traditions and practices make up your preparation for Easter each year, the focus—the point of it all—is Jesus.